including all

Home, School and Community
United in Education

Concepta Conaty

with a foreword by
Professor John Coolahan

Published 2002 by
Veritas Publications
7/8 Lower Abbey Street
Dublin 1
Ireland

Email publications@veritas.ie
Website www.veritas.ie

ISBN 1 85390 625 5

A catalogue record for this book is available from the British Library.

Veritas books are printed on paper made from the wood pulp of
managed forests. For every tree felled, at least one tree is planted,
thereby renewing natural resources.

Cover design by Pierce Design
Printed in the Republic of Ireland by Betaprint Ltd

contents

FOREWORD

WITHIN OUR FAST-CHANGING SOCIETY the role of the school has undergone great change. A striking feature of the change is the greater links between the school and the other educational partners or stakeholders. The rights and involvement of parents in relation to the school system have been transformed. Schools are now encouraged to have structured links with their local communities and the latter are urged to regard their schools as central to quality of life of the communities. Research has shown that the nature of individuals' experience of schooling has major repercussions for their life chances. Linked to their human resource development policies, in the context of lifelong learning, developed societies are now very keen to maximise the enrolment, retention and success levels of the young generation within the school system. Social inclusion became a key mantra in the nineties, giving rise to a great deal of attention by policy makers, researchers and practitioners to countering the incidence of social and educational disadvantage in society. It has been learned that the elimination of such disadvantage is a complex and multi-layered problem. It does not yield to single-focused initiatives, or to short-term interventions. It has been recognised that while schools have a role to play in the alleviation of the problem, to make real progress their efforts need to be supplemented by multi-faceted social interventions within the family and deprived local communities. The schools cannot provide a social panacea for deep-rooted problems, many of them outside the schools' control.

Over the last fifteen years or so, Ireland has given a much higher policy priority to tackling poverty and to targeting social and educational disadvantage than hitherto. A range of school-focused programmes such as Early Start, Breaking the Cycle, Early School Leavers Initiative, and School Retention Initiative have been instituted. Also, extra resources for disadvantaged schools and traveller education have been provided and there has been an expansion of resource teachers and the psychological service. The Area Partnerships, under the Area Development Management (ADM), have included education as part of their integrated approach to tackling the problems of local communities experiencing multi-layered forms of disadvantage. The Combat Poverty Agency, the Economic and Social Forum and a number of research studies have fostered a more sophisticated public awareness and understanding of the issues and problems involved. Arising from these, the Government adopted a National Anti-Poverty Strategy (NAPS). In 2001 a national committee on educational disadvantage, as provided for in the Education Act of 1998, was established. Many of the specific educational initiatives for which resources are earmarked in the National Development Plan are grouped within a social inclusion heading. These all betoken that contemporary Ireland, which has benefited from a decade of sustained economic growth, has indicated its concern that a 'two-nations syndrome' does not become entrenched for the future, with all the deleterious consequences that would entail.

Within this contextual framework, *Including All* provides us with the first authoritative and comprehensive account of one of the most significant interventions that has been made to tackle disadvantage – the Home/School/Community/Liaison Programme. This was begun as a pilot scheme from 1990 to 1993. Since then it has been developed, deepened and expanded to include post-primary as well as primary schools, and rural as well as urban settings. The book's author, Dr Concepta Conaty, has been with the project from the beginning, working in close association with the Department of Education and Science and the cohort of skilled personnel that has been trained to engage in this sophisticated initiative. While working within a carefully thought-out plan of action, the initiative reflects a wide range of best practice features of genuine partnership, as it operates in an unostentatious but efficient and effective manner. It has fostered bonds of good relationship and regard between school staffs, parents and local communities. One of its key aims is to empower disadvantaged parents by nurturing their capacity to engage as partners in the education of their children. There is no 'quick fix' solution to remedying deep-lying problems, but the enlightened, patient and sustained approach, which registers more in the hearts and personalities of those touched by the project than in media headlines, is the way forward. It is noteworthy that the OECD study, Parents as Partners in Schooling (1997), makes specific mention of Ireland's HSCL Scheme as 'a good example of innovative central government initiatives'. The report goes on to state, 'it is clear from the Irish experience that educational initiatives based in schools can raise the educational levels of the adults involved, and result in a general sense of empowerment in the local community. Parental involvement, especially in areas of socio-economic deprivation, does not just benefit the children and the school – it is a crucial aspect of lifelong learning' (p. 38). Such international endorsement, dating from 1997, would be likely to be even more affirmative if the study was conducted today, as the HSCL Scheme has developed a great deal since then.

The author is in an advantageous position to give us an insider's view of the project because of her long experience with it and the central role she has played in its implementation and development. Her skills, energies, commitment, enthusiasm and painstaking unselfishness of time and effort have been admired by those involved. A myriad of meetings, vast numbers of training sessions, much travelling, long nights of contact in many and varied locations, thousands of school visits, and so on, have been very much part of her input. These are not the issues emphasised in the book, nor is the author's own extraordinary effort noted. Thus, it would seem appropriate that a 'Foreword' should make mention of these aspects. A problem with an insider's view can sometimes be a too close, subjective engagement with the theme. The author has succeeded in avoiding this danger. As well as being a prime agent in the delivery of the programme, she also undertook a disciplined academic study of the programme, and this benefits her treatment of the theme.

Chapter one contextualises educational disadvantage within the recent history of the Irish education system. In chapter two the author draws on the insights of a range of theoreticians and practitioners on the best modes of intervention to tackle educational disadvantage and draws on the experience of a number of countries. The significance of the absence of a favourable home and community environment, particularly in areas of serious socio-economic disadvantage is clearly demonstrated. The next chapter presents us with a fascinating and detailed account of the Home/School/Community Liaison (HSCL) programme in Ireland, since its initiation in 1990. It sets out the principles that underpinned the scheme, the structure of the scheme and the roles of key protagonists, the training methods and processes, the emergent roles of parents and local communities. One gets an intimate sense of the pioneering aspects of the work, as new approaches are being developed within a patterned and traditional social scene. It is clear that great effort is put in to operationalise the scheme's values of prevention, integration and partnership.

In chapter four the author explores the concepts of partnership, power, authority and patriarchy, and empowerment. There is a particularly insightful treatment of partnership and an awareness that 'not only is time required to achieve partnership, but genuine implementation also takes time'. The attitudes of key participants in the programme are sought by questionnaire and interviews. Again, the key role of the coordinator and the sophisticated skills of the coordinators emerge as key linchpins of the programme. It emerges convincingly that teachers who have the right qualities and training are the ideal personnel for the liaison role in the HSCL Scheme.

Drawing on a wide range of pertinent literature, chapter five – 'Practical Steps', has much richness to offer to all involved in the process of education, as well as those with a more particular interest in HSCL. It highlights many features of the benign, progressive and effective school community in evolving contemporary society, as it relates pro-actively with its clients and partners. One also notes that the extensive bibliography should be of major interest to students and researchers in the field.

The final chapter reviews the strengths and weaknesses of the existing HSCL Scheme and gives valuable indications as to how the weaknesses can be addressed. It is clearly established that the three entities – home, school and community – need each other and the coordinator is seen as the key facilitator in bonding them. The author remarks, 'It is this centring of the role of the coordinator that makes the Irish scheme unique and one could argue an important development in educational theory and practice'. The author is well aware of the culture shift involved in parents and teachers working closely together, but it is impressive to learn that such co-operation on policy formation was a highly successful practice in 94 per cent of the HSCL schools in 1997-1998. The author quite rightly emphasises that the integrated delivery of service in marginalised communities is vital. She quotes from a Department of Education and Science statement, from the year 2000, that the HSCL Scheme 'is now the cornerstone and force for integration of service in all departmental strategies that are designed to address educational disadvantage and early school leaving'. In the light of this statement, *Including All* is a most timely and essential work for all those with interest in issues affecting the quality, inclusiveness and future of Irish education.

John Coolahan
NUI Maynooth

Preface

WE ARE LIVING in very exciting times in education. One of the advantages of the Celtic Tiger has been the availability of comparatively abundant resources and finance. We see a proliferation of new plans and initiatives. Many are at national level emanating from the Department of Education and Science, many are local.

It is recognised that there is a great need for structures, buildings, IT facilities and physical resources, and more will have to be provided in the years ahead.

But disturbingly, difficulties remain in education that cannot be solved merely by money. The resources needed are surely financial, but they are also the more intangible, but ultimately more significant people resources. In order to be solved, the educational problems of Irish society need people and their talents as much as they need government grants.

One of the more intractable problems is marginalisation. With all the undoubted goodwill among teachers and educational administrators, some pupils seem to slip through a net and fail to realise their potential. The failure should not be laid at the door of the children or their parents. It is not the pupils that fail, but the system.

In the past decade there have been some very important initiatives targeting marginalisation. Department policies and the commitment of recent Ministers for Education and Science have led to schemes that hold exciting promise for the future. I have been involved with these, both as a school principal from 1980 and from within the Department of Education and Science since 1990. This book has grown out of the experience of these years. The opinions expressed are my own and cannot necessarily be taken as representing official Government or Department positions, though I would hope that these would not be in conflict.

The key insight behind a lot of recent educational thinking is an awareness of the need to broaden the educational basis. The oft-repeated dictum that 'parents are the prime educators' has a serious meaning and cannot remain as a catch-cry or mere aspirational statement. Education is not something centred either in the home or in the school, but rather is to be seen as an ellipse in which there are two foci – the home and the school. This ellipse itself remains centred in the community.

The book introduces recent thinking on these three vital components of education: home, school and community. It traces initiatives taken in Ireland and elsewhere in bringing these to bear on the issue of marginalisation and offers some critique and evaluation of significant areas of Irish education.

A major conclusion of the book is that what is important for the problem of marginalisation has wider implications for the whole of education, at both primary and post-primary levels. Principles that are involved in the Home/School/Community Liaison Scheme (HSCL) such as partnership, respect for the individual as parent, pupil and teacher, interdependence, prevention, analysis of needs, integrated delivery of service, structures, the evaluation of initiatives – all of these have a relevance beyond the more immediate area of marginalisation.

When teachers and parents come into a full appreciation of the limits and possibilities of one another's role, the ensuing mutual understanding and trust could lead, perhaps, to a revolution in Irish education.

I take the opportunity of thanking those from whom I have learned so much: HSCL coordinators, teachers, parents and pupils nationally, and the authors whose ideas I have found so stimulating. I am particularly appreciative of the talent and dedication of my colleagues in the Department of Education and Science. I am very grateful, too, for the help I received from Professor John Coolahan during my years at Maynooth and for his readiness to accept the invitation of Veritas to write the 'Foreword' for *Including All*. I much appreciate the skill, accuracy and professionalism of my editor in Veritas, Helen Carr.

The material of this book was developed as a doctoral thesis under the direction of Dr Sheelagh Drudy (then a senior lecturer at Maynooth, now Professor of Education in University College Dublin) to whom I am very thankful. The thesis itself carried acknowledgement to many who assisted in its research and writing, and in particular to Rev. Dr Christopher O'Donnell, O. Carm., a theologian at the Milltown Institute, Dublin with whom I enjoyed tossing around ideas over many years.

Concepta Conaty

CHAPTER ONE

Marginalisation

IN THE DEVELOPED WORLD during the latter part of the twentieth century an enormous amount of money has been poured into education. There have been many positive results, such as increased literacy, employment, living standards and opportunities. The number attending second and third level continues to increase. However, in other ways, the fruits can be seen as disappointing. This poor response is most noticeable in areas marked by a wide range of socio-economic problems that at first sight may not seem to impinge on education. A clear example can be seen in the fact that the same child can experience two very different environments, one in his or her home surroundings and the other in school. Expectations, values and demands of the home and the school may be in conflict. This discontinuity or gap, which is psychological, social, spiritual and sometimes moral, is not sufficiently recognised in either educational theory or practice.

For the young person, failure is not merely a series of events such as tests and examinations, rather it is an environment in which the child is trapped. It can be difficult for parent, teacher or child to see a way out. Many of the young people who are not gaining maximum advantage from the available education today are themselves children of parents who were educationally disadvantaged. Such families can be found anywhere in rural or urban areas, but especially where there is not a social mix in housing and employment. They tend to cluster in densely populated urban areas, newly developed estates in large towns and, to a lesser degree, in dispersed rural areas.

It is a widely held fact that schools cannot address the multi-faceted nature of educational disadvantage on their own. Undoubtedly, the education system has a vital role to play. However, the school must incorporate the home in a partnership process within the wider context of community, including statutory and voluntary agencies.

Since 1990, the focus of the Department of Education (now the Department of Education and Science) has been characterised by a positive discrimination in favour of the most marginalised in designated areas of disadvantage. The advent of the Home/School/Community Liaison Scheme (HSCL) heralded this change. This scheme is the cornerstone and integrating factor of the Department's initiatives serving marginalised areas and of current programmes that address educational disadvantage and early school leaving.

The attempts to eradicate marginalisation have for us a threefold interest. Firstly, it is the story of an important area of education in Ireland. Secondly, it is an on-going history since disadvantage remains and strategies for dealing with it are continually evolving. Thirdly, the crucial importance of looking at how marginalisation has been tackled is not only a challenge, but also has important lessons – even the possibility of a Copernican revolution for Irish education. The strategies that have emerged, therefore, offer the possibility for a new vision for education at every socio-economic level in urban, town and rural areas.

Marginalisation/Disadvantage

The term 'disadvantage' is an ambiguous one. Policymakers view the notion from the point of view of defining programmes to promote social inclusion, educators grapple with the concept as it applies to traditional learning styles, while social scientists attend to its characteristics in order to identify populations for study.[1] The focus of all these groups would be to ease the effects of disadvantage on individuals and groups and, if possible, to break the cycle of poverty – particularly for children and teenagers. P. Archer, an Irish researcher and writer, holds that equality is achieved when a healthy blend of race, gender and social class prevails among the student and general population.[2]

A growing body of literature uses the terms 'disadvantaged', 'marginalised', 'at risk', 'deprived', 'underprivileged', and 'poor'. Irish researchers point to the fact that these terms are often used with few efforts at definition and often 'assumed to be equivalent in meaning'.[3] Educational disadvantage finds its roots in the wider context of socio-economic disadvantage.[4] It is unlikely that children can benefit from the educational system if the family is just surviving.[5]

Marginalised pupils may be described as frequently presenting in school with complex social, emotional, health and developmental needs that are barriers to learning. In addition, the marginalised pupils are most likely to be children and teenagers who come from homes where poverty exists to such a degree as to preoccupy the family and to affect its ability to enhance life chances. They are generally young people from the families of the unskilled and the unemployed working-class, with a history of educational failure. As a result, these young people have fewer choices in life, have limited access to further education and so have less opportunity to realise their potential.[6] The American researcher, L. Schorr advises that

Virtually all of the other risk factors that make rotten outcomes more likely are found disproportionately among poor children: bad health in infancy and childhood, being abused or neglected, not having a decent place to live, and lacking access to services that protect against the effect of these conditions.[7]

In marginalised areas, there is often a reduced ability to cope within the home and the community, thus creating oppression and perpetuating the cycle of disadvantage, early school leaving and educational failure. Families with these characteristics generally live in densely populated urban areas. They are also found in dispersed rural communities, but to a lesser degree. In such situations, equality of opportunity is lacking, social exclusion is prolonged and there is a serious loss of talent to society. This inability often finds expression in apathy, voicelessness, vandalism, substance misuse, joy-riding, demotivation, low self-image and alienation.

In short we can say that under-achievement in school, unsatisfactory retention rates and a poor accessing of higher education led the Department of Education to initiate a scheme of special funding in 1984 for schools in designated areas of disadvantage.

Solutions to the needs of marginalised pupils require a range of services and supports that cut across the boundaries of the school, agency services – both statutory and voluntary – and government departments. Solutions also include the involvement of parents and the development of communities to provide stable, safe and supportive environments for young people. This comprehensive range of provisions and the ensuing good practice would seem to be the way forward in addressing the needs of those 'at risk'. When home, school and community, together with voluntary and statutory services, are treated in isolation there is a limited chance of success. A partnership, a multi-agency approach may be the path to follow.

Socio-economic and educational disadvantage, including 'uninvolved' parents, have been under discussion in educational circles across the developed and developing world since the early 1960s. Disadvantage is central for two reasons. Firstly, it is an issue emerging, studied and responded to worldwide. Most specifically, as we will see, the Home/School/Community Liaison Scheme (HSCL) emerged from the Department of Education precisely in answer to deprivation and need.

Traditional theories have held that a pupil is disadvantaged if he/she belongs to a minority group, a low-income group or a group with low educational status. A more recent addition is the theory that relates disadvantage to the self-image, incorporating self-worth and self-confidence, which the individual has of himself/herself. In the *Educational Researcher*, five key indicators are associated with the educationally disadvantaged: 'minority racial/ethnic group identity, living in a poverty household, living in a single-parent family, having a poorly educated mother, and having a non-English language background'.[8] The authors hold that some children may be classified as educationally disadvantaged when a number of these indicators relate to the same family.[9] In Ireland, the indicators of disadvantage in designated areas are related to the type of housing pupils live in, the number of pupils whose families hold medical cards and are in receipt of unemployment benefit. In addition, the level of education of the mother, followed by that of the father, is taken into consideration.[10]

The Irish Endeavour within a European and World Context

In order to build a 'learning society', the European White Paper on education and training postulates five general objectives, one of them being to combat social exclusion. The White

Paper highlights the fact that 'Schools located in the 'problem' areas are increasingly reorganizing ... by using the best teachers, better paid than elsewhere, an appropriate teaching pace, in-company placements, multimedia equipment and smaller classes ... Another aim must be to turn the school – in problem areas where social and family values are generally collapsing – into an educational meeting place where teachers are present outside school hours'.[11]

At the UN World Summit in Copenhagen in March 1995, the Irish Government endorsed a programme of action aimed at eliminating absolute poverty in the developing world and reducing overall poverty and inequality everywhere. Arising from this commitment, the Irish Government approved the development of a National Anti-Poverty Strategy (NAPS) that would address poverty, exclusion and inequality, and ensure coordination across and between departments and involve people directly affected by poverty.

Regarding educational disadvantage, the overall objective of NAPS is 'to ensure that children, men and women living in poverty are able to gain access, participate in and benefit from education of sufficient quality to allow them to move out of poverty, and to prevent others from becoming poor'.[12] Strategies in education were identified to achieve this objective. They included eliminating barriers to participation in education for welfare dependent families and supporting lifelong learning and community-based education and training. The provision of pre-school education, the prevention of educational disadvantage through extension of the HSCL Scheme and the integration of the school and community dimension of provision were stated. The reduction of class size, a continuum of provision for special education and working to include travellers in primary and post-primary education were named.

In the reviews of NAPS[13] it would seem that the Global Target, that of reducing consistent poverty in Ireland to 5 to 10 per cent by 2007, has been achieved. The NAPS targets on unemployment have already been realised and superseded. However, the realisation of the education target, the elimination of early school leaving before the Junior Certificate and the retention figure of 90 per cent to Leaving Certificate by 2000 and 98 per cent by 2007, have proved more problematic. A statutory framework to address poor school attendance, underachievement and early school leaving is provided through the Education (Welfare) Act, 2000. An Educational Welfare Board has been instituted in order to ensure that each child attends a recognised educational establishment up to sixteen years of age, or accesses an adequate level of education. Education Welfare Officers will be appointed to work closely with schools, the relevant statutory providers and families to ensure continuance in education.

The second element of the education target is to ensure that literacy and numeracy problems would not present in early primary education by 2002. This aspect has received less concentration than the retention issue, but according to the Combat Poverty Agency it is just as important.[14] Indeed, a wide body of educational research into early childhood, including the work of the Bernard van Leer Foundation,[15] points to the significance of early years learning.

School Retention

H. Johnston, an American educator on secondary school issues, claims that to retain pupils in school 'specific and careful attention needs to be given to the early perceptions of the institution formed by incoming youth'.[16] There are clear advantages for young people whose parents have had lengthy exposure to second and third-level education. These are outlined by K. Lynch, who holds that the educated middle class are able to maximise the benefits of the educational system.[17] One might ask if our schools transform and/or reproduce social inequalities.

Disadvantaged young people often fail to do the required work to ensure high achievement. R. Clark, a consultant to school systems working on improving home-school relations, advises that it is challenging for educators to ensure that learning is a stimulating process.[18] In *Schooling for Change* we note that 'too many of our students are turning away from schools physically, or tuning out of them emotionally and intellectually'.[19] These Canadian writers hold that when teenagers are

> most in need of care and support ... we focus on teaching subject matter ... and leave students' emotional needs to the peer group and the gang ... Early adolescents need independence but we show them indifference. They need kindness but we crush them with control. They are brimming with criticism and curiosity, but we bludgeon them with content and its coverage.[20]

The European White Paper on Education holds that 'education must be opened up to the world of work ... companies must be involved in the training drive ... cooperation must be developed between schools and firms and new avenues must be explored for the validation of skills'.[21] Perhaps the introduction of a modular Leaving Certificate in Ireland would allow marginalised pupils, who find it so difficult to adapt to the current school structure, the opportunity to join the work force and to study to certification. It is possible for graduates to attain post-graduate qualifications and to continue in a full-time capacity in the world of work. Why not a similar opportunity for our marginalised young people?

The requirements of our disadvantaged are highlighted in the following statistics, so too is the urgent need for change in the educational system so that schools may adapt to the needs of the marginalised as opposed to the expectation that the marginalised must always adapt to the needs of the school. The extent of educational disadvantage in Ireland is observable from the following statistics relating to post-primary pupils during the 1993-1995 school year:

- up to 1,000 did not progress to second level school
- 3,000 left second level school with no qualification
- 7,600 left school having completed Junior Certificate only, of which 2,400 failed to achieve at least five passes in the Junior Certificate
- 2,600 young people left school having completed the Junior Certificate and the Vocational Preparatory Training course only
- around 7,000 did not achieve five passes in the Leaving Certificate[22]

(A further challenge for educators is to view ability as multifaceted and incremental, and to validate without reducing standards.) This calls for a major shift in thinking from the view that only academic qualifications are of merit. The Irish Government, and in particular the Department of Education, has focused on the need of marginalised pupils. Policy changes have been initiated. The alteration of school structures and practices, a more enlightened and positive way of viewing both marginalised pupils and their families and effective schooling are called for.

Retention of pupils is a problem for many schools in designated areas of disadvantage. The language used in literature and in schools requires examination. So too does the concept of single policy action. Labelling all departures from school as 'dropouts' may cast all the blame on the pupil when, in fact, schools may need to look at alternative ways of working. Equally, not all forms of departure can be addressed by the school. It may even be the case that mistargeting of services will prove counterproductive in the long-term.[23]

Ultimately, Tinto argues that effective retention lies not necessarily in the types of programmes provided for pupils but in the underlying commitment that inspires staff.[24]

It is useful to note that membership of the school is based on social bonding. American research has described the four elements of social bonding as attachment, commitment, involvement and belief.[25] Pupils were socially bonded to the extent that they attached to adults and peers, were committed to the ethos of the school and were involved in school activities with a belief in the legitimacy of schooling. They argue that it is the 'dropout who questions the efficacy of schooling because it does not appear to lead to his or her valued goals'[26] – what a challenging statement for all educators. These American researchers further add that there is evidence to support the fact that most pupils started school with the expectation of completing it.[27]

Obviously, the more parents know about the school the more they can contribute to their children's schooling. The committed pupil remains in school to graduation, spurred on by internalised goals emanating from the home, the school and wider society. What about the pupil who comes from a home disrupted by poverty, unemployment, relationship difficulties and substance misuse? This question leads us into the next section dealing with Department of Education schemes for marginalised pupils and their families.

Department of Education Initiatives in Ireland

Initiatives have been in place for decades to help disadvantaged pupils at primary level, for example the school meals service and the free-book/book-rental scheme. In 1984 a more focused approach became apparent with the introduction of a programme of special measures for schools in disadvantaged areas of Dublin, Cork and Limerick with a *per capita* grant to principals at primary level for books and materials. A further grant was sent to the chairperson to encourage home, school and community liaison. In evaluation carried out by the Department of Education in 1985/1986 and again in 1987/1988 schools reported an impact from a morale and financial point of view. However, very little had happened regarding parent involvement. During the period 1984-1990 concessionary posts were allocated to most schools in disadvantaged areas and these schools were also favoured in the granting of remedial teachers.

At post-primary level, curriculum adaptation to meet the needs of the less academic pupil was a commitment of the Irish Government in the White Paper on Educational Development (1980). This started with the reform of the Intermediate Certificate, re-named the Junior Certificate, with a further adaptation in 1996 to the Junior Certificate Schools' Programme, suited to the less academic pupil. The Leaving Certificate went through even more stages in its development to the Leaving Certificate Applied (LCA). The LCA is currently in operation and apparently more suited to some children from lower socio-economic backgrounds. Post-primary schools serving disadvantaged pupils have at least one ex-quota post for remedial teaching. Primary and post-primary schools in designated areas of disadvantage receive a higher *per capita* grant than the non-designated schools.

Throughout the 1990s, a number of pilot projects were initiated to test models of service delivery to educationally marginalised children and their families. The HSCL Scheme led the way in 1990. It was followed by the Early Start Pre-school

Project which is a provision for three-year old children in forty selected schools in designated areas of disadvantage. Early Start has a pupil-teacher ratio of fifteen to one, has significant resources and has specified behavioural outcomes. There are strong bonds between HSCL coordinators, parents, teachers and child-care workers in Early Start.

Breaking the Cycle, (BTC) urban and rural dimensions, was introduced in 1996. The urban dimension, with a total of thirty-two schools, has a fifteen to one pupil-teacher ratio in the first four years of schooling. There are one hundred and twenty-two schools in the rural dimension. The schools are clustered into groups and have the services of a teacher-coordinator whose role resembles that of the HSCL coordinator, but with the addition of a teaching element. The HSCL and BTC coordinators work closely together at local level.

The Support Teacher Project deploys teachers to work with children who are disturbed, disruptive and withdrawn. The HSCL coordinator works with parents while the Support Teacher works with the child. The quality of outcome for the child may be very much enhanced through the integration of schemes and projects.

The 8-15 Early School Leaver Initiative (ESLI) was designed to test models of integrated service formulated to meet the need of 'at risk' pupils. In-school, out-of-school and holiday provision took place with assistance from the formal and the non-formal sectors.[28] The Stay in School Retention Initiative (SSRI) focused on the areas with the highest level of early school leaving and its work practices are very similar to those of ESLI. It makes a lot of sense that ESLI and SSRI will soon be subsumed into the School Completion Programme (SCP). The School Completion Programme will come into focus with the forthcoming expansion of the service to the marginalised, and should be up and running by summer 2002. The HSCL

Scheme, ESLI and SSRI have, and always have had, very close working relationships. This is part of their combined strength and is evidenced by the way in which National and Assistant National Coordinators work in tandem. It is also obvious at home, school and community levels where local personnel in the different initiatives work so well together in providing an integrated delivery of service to marginalised young people and their families-communities.

The HSCL Scheme, which was established in 1990 in designated areas of disadvantage, is the main focus of this book (see Chapter Three). It is a commitment by the Department of Education to develop the parent as prime educator. In addition, it seeks to promote change in school attitudes and behaviours so that parents and teachers can work in partnership to help realise the potential of 'at risk' pupils. It can be said that the HSCL Scheme was, and is, about radical change, change in the way people think, plan, learn, act and evaluate – particularly in the school context.

The HSCL Scheme is a targeted and focused resource, aimed at the most marginalised within the designated schools. This is positive discrimination in favour of the most marginalised or 'positive differential treatment in which some students are seen as different in some educationally relevant way, and are treated differently from others out of respect for fairness'[29]. The designated primary schools, on the whole, serve a 100 per cent marginalised catchment area. However, this is not the case with the post-primary schools. In many instances, within the scheme, the post-primary school serves only a 20 to 25 per cent marginalised catchment. In such schools, a choice has to be made by the coordinator, (the teacher from the staff who works in a full-time capacity with the significant adults in the pupil's life – see Chapters Three and Four), in consultation with the principal, regarding which families are to receive the

HSCL service. Generally speaking, the relevant families have passed through the 'feeder' primary schools which are designated.

Not only is the HSCL Scheme a targeted and focused resource, it is also a preventative and integrated service. 'Prevention' has been highlighted by the HSCL Scheme since its inception in 1990. The concept of prevention has been further recommended by the National Economic and Social Forum (NESF)[30]. The large volume of research available today points to the fact that prevention is less expensive and more productive than are the treatment and attempts at solution when the problems have emerged. The 'emphasis should be on habilitation rather than rehabilitation, on self determined change rather than on the cure of some supposed disease'.[31]

This chapter serves as a brief introduction to the problems in Irish education, to a definition of marginalisation/ educational disadvantage and its reality for young people and their families.

CHAPTER TWO

Attempts to Deal with Marginalisation

THE LAST TWENTY years, and in particular the last decade, have been an exciting and demanding time in education. One aspect of the change has been the gradual move from the separation of home and school to an increasing acceptance of the central role of the parent as prime educator. In recent times there has also been much emphasis on the role of the community as a central one in learning.

It will be the contention of this book that in Ireland there have been important developments in the three areas of home, school and community and above all in their interrelationships. It would be foolhardy to try to give a single cause for this new interest in the interrelatedness of home, school and community, but one generalisation can perhaps be risked. A significant catalyst has been the perception that education was failing, especially in the more disadvantaged socio-economic areas. This perception was supported by much theoretical work, which gave increased relevance and urgency to the problem in the last two decades. Some of the theoretical work, which dates from the late 1950s, viewed low-income people as 'culturally deprived' and requiring 'compensatory education'. A patronising tone prevailed among educators who approached the learning of working-class people with insensitivity and with middle class prejudices. Movements in the mid-1980s have placed more emphasis on home-school relationships and the 1990s have seen the inclusion of community as part of the focus.

We shall examine this phenomenon within the work of educationalists. The interdependent and integrated nature of learning from a home, community and school perspective will be highlighted. Parallels will also be drawn and lessons will be learned from a worldwide vantage point. Attitudes of teachers and other professionals towards parents will be assessed.

The Views of Leading Educators

The upsurge in interest in the triple direction of home, school, and community is a relatively new phenomenon. On the one hand there are many studies on each of the elements; on the other hand the interdependence of all three is not nearly so well investigated, although there are many studies on any two of the three.

When we look at projects and studies we find four different kinds of significant contribution to this debate. There are foundational, political, and social principles in national and transnational bodies. Secondly, there are theoretical and practical studies by educationalists. Thirdly, there are initiatives taken by governments and educational authorities of a practical and sometimes a theoretical nature. Finally, there are studies of individual initiatives here and abroad. In this book a thematic approach has been chosen and the four different approaches are presented under five headings.

The Rights of Parents

The renewed emphasis on the rights of parents can be seen in the context of an insistence in the twentieth century on human rights in world organisations, in constitutional law and generally in politics, philosophy and ethics. Teachers often underrate the rights and the role of parents, and indeed, so do parents themselves. 'The status and role of parents is ignored by society until ... official attention by virtue of perceived and apparent problems with the child-rearing process (emerge)'.[1]

Bunreacht na h-Éireann (The Irish Constitution), has a clear expression of the rights and responsibilities of parents: 'The State acknowledges that the primary and natural educator of the child is the Family and guarantees to respect the inalienable right and duty of parents to provide, according to their means for the religious and moral, intellectual, physical and social education of their children'.[2]

The European Convention on Human Rights ensures the right to education and assures parents that such education will be 'in conformity with their own religious and philosophical convictions'.[3]

The education section of the Maastricht Treaty, Article 126, states that:

> The Community shall contribute to the development of quality education by encouraging co-operation between member States and, if necessary, by supporting and supplementing their action, while fully respecting the responsibility of the Member States for the content of teaching and the organization of education systems and their cultural and linguistic diversity.[4]

The Treaty wishes the Community to pursue 'co-operation between educational establishments'. A Scottish educator A. Macbeth and a Danish colleague, B. Ravn, suggest that the two basic educational establishments for any child are home and school and that 'cooperation between the two could be adopted as a major Community interest'.[5] Such co-operation was envisaged and intended to be implemented with the setting up of primary school Boards of Management in Ireland in 1975. Boards of Management were established to allow a wider participation by trustees, parents and teachers in the shared management of schools.

> The fundamental question is whether appropriate adjustments and adaptations can be made to bring the governance of schools into line with the very changed economic, social, and political circumstances…winning the allegiance of the relevant partners…[with] increasing demands for more democratic participation of parents and teachers in the governance of our schools.[6]

The shared management of schools, in the real sense, has been slow. An earlier criticism of the management of national schools being 'little more than a minor maintenance committee' has been warranted.[7] It emerges from talking to school personnel and to parents that, generally speaking, Boards of Management do not deal with curriculum planning, implementation and review, nor with the critical issue of the non-performing teacher.[8] The Green Paper (government policy statement intended for discussion) on Education advocated that 'much more authority and responsibility be devolved to local level'.[9] The National Parents Council – Primary (NPC-P) has, in a publication for parents, made many recommendations to enhance the effective participation of parents on boards.[10] Despite structures for their inclusion, parents have been reluctant to exercise their rights and avail of opportunities. It would appear, from speaking to parents and school personnel, and from research findings, that the participation of parents is often consigned to their having a merely peripheral role.[11] A former Minister for Education admits 'lack of knowledge by parents may inhibit them from going forward to serve on boards, deprive them of the experience of partnership ... and the children of the school of the benefit of their participation'.[12] In the White Paper (indicating proposed legislation)

> The Government is committed to promoting the active participation of parents at every level of the education process. It also supports the right of parents to be consulted, as part of a collaborative process for educational decision- and policy-making at school, regional and national level ... This formal recognition will be given statutory confirmation.[13]

In every school in receipt of Exchequer funding 'a statutory duty will be placed on boards of management to promote the setting up by parents of a parents' association'.[14] Reiterating the stance taken by the Minister for Education in 1991 in her circular 'Parents as Partners in Education',[15] the White Paper states that 'each board of management will be required to develop a formal home-school links policy ... stating the actions which will be taken to foster such links'.[16] The Education Act (1998) enshrined the foregoing in law.[17]

It is evident that successive ministers worked to include the parent voice both at board level and through parent associations. A further effort at inclusion was through the intended Education Boards. When the establishment of Education Boards, which would have operated as an intermediate tier between the Department of Education and school boards was proposed, the Minister intended 'that the autonomy of schools would be enhanced'.[18]

A recent study of the characteristics of the Department of Education point to the fact that its centralised nature and detailed work with individuals prevent adequate attention to policy matters.[19]

From the foregoing views of the Irish Constitution, the European Convention on Human Rights, the Maastricht Treaty and the Irish Government Department of Education it is clear that the role given to parents is of paramount importance. Boards of Management give parents an opportunity for wider participation. The National Parents' Council encourages participation. The White Paper advocates the 'active participation of parents at every level'. The 1998 Education Act concretises the role of the parent in education. It would appear that much work needs to be done to provide a climate of support for parents and teachers and to enable parents to assume their rights. A British educationalist, S. Wolfendale, calls for greater participation of parents so 'that the proper exercising of citizens' rights would extend to parents having a greater share in educational decision-making on behalf not only of their children, but in true community spirit on behalf of all adult citizens of tomorrow'.[20]

Home-based Learning and Social Class

There is a long recognised relationship between home background and in-school attainment. Much of the recent debate has centred on the adequacy or otherwise of working-class families. The discussion has taken place within a wider sociological and economic framework, together with an awareness of the inequality that persists despite many improvements in prosperity, in welfare, and in education.[21] In his work *Early Childhood Education and Care*, W. Barker – who has been involved in evaluative work in Britain and Ireland – cautioned that unless there is 'equal valuing and learning of skills and concepts drawn from the culture of the disadvantaged, the disadvantaged child's self-esteem is damaged and its potential for development … seriously inhibited'.[22]

There have been different views about the value of home background and children's learning, particularly in the area of language development. Some decades ago B. Bernstein[23] postulated two polar codes in relation to language development, the 'elaborated' and the 'restricted' based on middle and working-class homes. He considered that the latter was 'deficit' in language. However, his theory has been 'developed and refined over a long period of time'.[24] P. Widlake, a former teacher, teacher trainer, researcher and founder editor of the journal *Remedial Education* refutes the notion of restricted codes in marginalised areas. He highlights the 'conceptual crudity and confusion' of such thought when he speaks of 'the patronising tone that prevailed among educators … [their] insensitivity … the reinforcement of teachers' middle class prejudices; the denigration of the language and mores of disadvantaged people'.[25] Two Irish educators, S. Drudy and K. Lynch, 'emphatically reject any explanation that rests on a deficit model of the children of the poor, as deficit theory is based on untenable assumptions about the superiority of one set of cultural values *vis-à-vis* others'.[26]

B. Tizard and M. Hughes, British authors, who have studied young children, contend that the main difference in language use occurs not between middle and working-class children, but between home and school. They conclude 'that children who are said to enter school hardly able to talk are almost always children who can talk perfectly well at home, but are initially too ill at ease to display the full range of their verbal skills when they enter school.'[27] Tizard and Hughes report two reasons why relatively little research has been done on home-based learning because 'the researcher must actually go into a child's home and observe what is happening there'.[28] Their second reason is of a very different nature and is 'the belief in some quarters that there is not much to be gained from attempting to do so. In other words, their reluctance has been due to the general belief that mothers, have very little to offer … this attitude may be partly due to the lowly non-professional status which parenting is frequently given'.[29]

The research findings of Tizard and Hughes suggest that the reverse is true, 'it was clear from our observations that the home provides a very powerful learning environment'.[30] In their book, *Young Children Learning*, they cite five reasons why the home is an especially effective learning environment. First, the range of activities is more extensive in the home than in the school. Second, the shared life in the home enables the mother to encourage the child 'to make sense of her present experiences by relating them to past experiences, as well as to her existing framework of knowledge'.[31] A third significant point is that a small number of children share the adults' time and attention in the home. A further characteristic is that learning 'is often embedded in contexts of great meaning to the child'.[32] Finally the relationship between mother and child is so close that 'she will almost certainly have definite educational expectations which she is likely to pursue ... it is this parental concern that converts the potential advantages of the home into actual advantages'.[33] A leading expert in the area of early childhood in the poorest stratum of American life, U. Bronfenbrenner, expresses the same sentiments and advocates home intervention in the early years. He focuses not on the child but on the mother-child relationship 'the two person system which sustains and fosters the child's development'.[34] The findings of Tizard and Hughes apply to both working-class and middle-class homes. The emphasis and content were sometimes different in the two sectors, yet 'all the basic language usages were observed in all the homes; the social class difference was in the frequency of the usages'.[35]

While it would seem wrong to conclude that different forms of language reflect inferior or superior modes of cognition or of thinking, Kellaghan and others 'assume that differences in values, beliefs, language and knowledge may be due ... to differences in the basic conditions of life at different levels of the social order'.[36] In addition, experience teaches that families within any socio-economic group vary considerably. The performance of children at school also varies. The explanatory value of such variables as parent education or occupation is limited since they tell us little about life in the home that might enhance the development of the child in school. However, research carried out from 1975 to 1979 in a disadvantaged area of London, designed to assess the effects of parental involvement in teaching reading, showed that 'children who receive parental help are significantly better in reading attainment than comparable children who do not ... [and that] small-group instruction in reading, given by a highly competent specialist teacher, did not produce improvements in attainment comparable in magnitude with those obtained from the collaboration with parents'.[37]

In another study the absence of 'problem behaviour in the home' had a substantial positive relationship with attention, the latter having moderate effects on arithmetic achievement and reading comprehension'.[38]

Processes in the home that are considered to play an important part in child development include the involvement of the parents with their children, their level of communication and general organisation within the home.[39] In Britain, G. Wells, writing about the acquisition of language, points out that conversations at home 'arise spontaneously from the activity in hand, and are free from any pressure to teach and learn particular facts and skills'.[40] Conversations of this nature are natural interactions with a family member. J. Goode, a British educator, analyses the nature of learning at home and offers a typology of 'parents as educators' within a three-fold framework: 'confirmatory', 'complementary' and 'compensatory'.[41] Macbeth sees home-based learning as a corollary to school-based learning, 'a mutual information exchange'.[42] He claims that the terms 'home background' and 'socio-economic' are broad and vague but that 'parental attitudes emerged as important variables correlating with achievement ... Social class itself is not the cause of inequalities of school performance but attitudes which may themselves correlate with socio-economic status could be having impact and it is in relation to these that action would be directed'.[43]

When trapped in poverty and in close contact with language development among low income people, P. Freire, a noted Brazilian educator remarked that 'Their syntax was as beautiful as mine ... they could never say what critical analysts know about language and social class'.[44] Similarily, Widlake is highly critical of how difficult children and tough neighbourhoods were first thought of as deficient, and then later as diffident.[45] Widlake works from 'compensatory education' through the 'communications model' to the 'participatory model' where 'parents are viewed ... as people exercising some control over their own lives ... and education of their children ... The very thought of these people being verbally destitute is enough to reduce one to helpless laughter'.[46] When teaching pupils 'in poverty' in an Australian primary school it has been observed that 'teachers, in the main, adopt derogatory, deficit views of their students and their families ... they are said to come from "bad families", which are poor and characterised as unstable and unsupportive of the school'.[47] Drudy and Lynch hold that there may be 'cultural discontinuities' between the home, community or school for working-class children but 'in no sense has it been proved that there is any deficit in the linguistic skills of these children'.[48] They go on to point out that recent research suggests that such children have 'verbal skills well in excess of their performance levels' and that 'schools themselves are the inhibiting force'.[49] Their suggested recommendation is 'to develop the language skills of children from culturally diverse backgrounds'.[50]

According to a study examining the likely course of change in disadvantaged populations in America between 1986 and 2020, minority racial/ethnic group status is perhaps the best known factor associated with educational disadvantage. The study claimed that 'members of certain minority groups have performed more poorly in schools than white children'.[51] It also held that the results from the National Assessment of Educational Progress showed that 'the reading and writing skills of black and Hispanic children were substantially below those of white children'.[52]

Crediting his parents for providing him with the 'social skills' and 'confidence' to take advantage of educational opportunities, J.P. Comer, a black psychiatrist, believed that teachers did not realise how 'afraid' and 'uncomfortable' black parents were around 'white people in general'.[53] In addition, teachers 'assume that all children come from mainstream backgrounds and arrive at school equally well prepared to perform as the school expects them to'.[54] He concludes that parent involvement in 'low-income communities … can help eliminate harmful stereotypes that staff members may harbour about the communities served by their school'.[55]

The discontinuity between the home and school life of children[56] has to be addressed at school level because 'continuity … reduces conflict for children, reinforces learning and eases the transition between the two environments'.[57] The discontinuity theory is based on the premise that an environment fosters the development of competencies that have adaptive value for individuals living in it.[58] Success in adapting to a new environment will depend on the ability of the individual to transfer learning. Homes and schools differ in their training and expectations so children will experience some difficulty in the transfer from home to school and from primary school to the post-primary sector.[59] In Ireland, the Conference of Major Religious Superiors, (CMRS) now called the Conference of Religious of Ireland, (CORI) have taken up the 'discontinuity' issue and that of 'deficit and difference'.[60]

Discontinuity can be eased by an overlap in home and school experiences. This can take place in the home by providing the child with school-related experiences and in school by teachers 'taking account, in their teaching of the categories of meaning that children bring with them of school'.[61] Caution is expressed that the pursuance of home-school links can only be 'within the context of a complex set of traditions, value assumptions and attitudes regarding the roles and relationships of family and society, individual and State'.[62] For D. Seeley, with a background in law and education, this way of working constitutes a partnership that is 'conducive to successful learning' where those involved share 'common effort toward common goals' and 'none is ever a client because their relationship is mutual'.[63]

In this section we have examined the debate relating to home-based learning and social class. We have highlighted many authors who have refuted the 'deficit' model of language development relating to the working-class home. The 'discontinuity' between the home life of the child and that at school was discussed. Various authors were used to show how an overlap in home and school experiences could ease the discontinuity.

Community-based Learning

'Community' is a word that we find constantly in sociological and educational literature. It is not without ambiguity. For the purpose of clarification we can take up the two types of community identified by Tönnies and Cooley about the turn of the century and known as the *Gemeinschaft* and *Gesellschaft* models. The former is the close-knit community with much face to face interaction where people are known, not just by name, but in their circumstances and their relationships. The notion of *Gemeinschaft* in the classification of Tönnies was further developed by Cooley in a description of 'primary groups'. The chief characteristics of a primary group are 'face to face association, the unspecialised character of that association, relative permanence, the small number of persons involved and the relative intimacy among the participants'.[64] The family, the old fashioned neighbourhood, the rural townland would be examples of such community. The *Gesellschaft* is the model of community that one finds in institutions where people may be known by name and by their function. An example of *Gesellschaft* is a human association characterised by formal organisational structures and office such as the secular state, the school, the hospital and the hotel. The organisation is maintained by competent authority, which is normally institutionalised in the form of an office. Such societies are governed by explicit rules, often written.[65] It would seem likely that contemporary educational theory would not be happy to see a school merely as an institutionalised society, *Gesellschaft*, whilst recognising at the same time that community in the sense of *Gemeinschaft* is liable to raise unrealistic expectations.[66]

A British writer, E. Midwinter, claims that those involved in education must push out the frontiers of the educative dimension to include 'universalisms' i.e. television, the pop culture, sports and advertising. He continues 'that whether teachers like it or not, the community at large 'educates'; 'community' in this sense is definable as the child's common wealth of experiences'.[67] The same idea is promoted by Bronfenbrenner who had as his central thesis the importance of contextual child development and the need to confront the total life situation of the child. He moved from a child-centred approach to a family-centred one. He recommends that parents, the extended family, school and community personnel are all vital to the socialisation of the child.[68] In this type of setting 'the nation's children can develop into constructive, contributing members of culture and society'.[69] There is little doubt regarding the place of the home and community in the life of the child. The Bernard van Leer Foundation (BvLF) strongly holds that

> The bond between parent and child should be the central pivot of educational activities ... the community has to perceive a commitment to educational change, not for the benefit of the outsiders, but for itself and its children ... Teachers for their part must know the cultural access-point in the local community. If they do not, they run the grave risk of failing the child and the community they pretend to address.[70]

In a significant study, *School Power*, we learn how a university, a public school and parents worked together to move problem inner city schools in New Haven to an acceptable level of social and academic achievement. The American author, J. P. Comer, sought to build a 'happy stable home environment' and 'cohesive supportive communities'.[71] Comer's belief is that this is fundamental to the development of the individual child and hence to family and to community life.[72] It can be expected that improved quality life across many families leads to an enriched community. J. MacBeath, a British educator and writer, (not to be confused with the Scottish educationalist Alastair Macbeth) advises that 'it is the nature of the movement between the communities of school and home that shapes the present and sets out the pathway to individual futures'.[73] Welling expresses the same sentiment: 'if we are really going to make an impact on the well-being of children growing up in deprived communities it is the totality of their environment which has to be addressed. The message is empowerment... We have to address not only the immediate provision for children but the disabling environment itself'.[74] In an American journal, *Phi Delta Kappan* we read of 'Neighbourhood Organisations that Keep Hope Alive', yet the authors speak chillingly about the difficulty young people experience 'when school doors shut behind them in the early afternoon'.[75] These pupils are 'claimed by the streets' where 'ill-equipped parks become urban battlegrounds'.[76]

In her development work in India R. Paz learned that 'communities are untapped reservoirs of human potential'[77] and for early childhood programmes to succeed they must be 'rooted in the community'.[78] This presumes an understanding of the community in which they are rooted. Summarising what she learned in programmes that were successful in breaking the cycle of disadvantage, an American, L. Schorr states 'Successful programs see the child in the context of family and the family in the context of its surroundings'.[79] Welling holds that just as children need healthy and strong bodies, they equally need healthy and strong supporting communities and concludes 'we are in the business of community development just as much as we are in the business of child development'.[80] The value of an integrated approach is further highlighted: 'the importance of family supports, school responsiveness to students, and student involvement in school and community activities stand out as predictors of recovery of low performance'.[81]

The task of education is to provide meaningful and relevant learning opportunities for children, parents and the wider community. This enhances the quality of life, thereby allowing children to grow up in an enriched environment, partaking of educational opportunity in ever increasing quality, depth and duration. In such a setting the child is being supported in educational endeavour. The child, the main target of intervention, occupies a central part of programmes with 'parents and the community in concentric circles of belonging and support, reinforcing and gaining sustenance from each other'.[82] In this way education can be seen as a process that is 'lifelong' where participants are 'actively and influentially' involved and where needs identification 'determines the nature and timing of the provision'.[83] Above all, the process is about 'working with, not for', is participatory, and builds on the existing strengths of the individual and of the community.[84] Commonly accepted values would seem to be an irreversible acquisition in educational theory. However, the practical translation of theory to practice will always remain a challenge. As noted above, we need to take some care that we do not raise unrealisable expectations in the way in which we speak about community and the importance of the individual. It remains a challenge and over enthusiastic language can lead to frustration, anger, or disillusionment.

Perhaps the successful schools of the future will be defined 'as those in which children, students, parents and teachers have learned how to learn together within a coherent theory of community education'.[85] MacBeath leaves those who may not be convinced of the interrelatedness of school and community with a disturbing question: 'what is the difference between "success" for a school and "success" for the individual who passes through it on the way to a lifetime in the community?'.[86]

School-based Learning

In many parts of the world the school and education are almost correlative terms. The automatic assumption of former times that education is primarily a school matter and that school is primarily the educator is now being tested and expanded and at times challenged. The challenge to previously held orthodoxy arises partly from educationalists and social commentators like Freire,[87] who begin not with theories, but from the experience of disappointing results from school-based learning and from the assumptions that the school is not only a primary locus of education, but almost an exclusive one. Another awareness is that the school is more than the classroom: the social skills learned in the playground are a primary element in the educational process, one which continues beyond the school walls.

Macbeth tells us that less than 15 per cent of a child's waking life from birth to sixteen years is spent in school, where learning is 'planned, structured, professionally provided and delivered at times of the day when children are alert and receptive'.[88] Two aspects of Freirean theory are relevant here. Firstly, the 'banking model', where ideas and information are 'put into' people's heads, rather like depositing money in a bank. Secondly, the 'problem-posing one' where the learner is actively and influentially involved. The Irish Primary School Curriculum of 1971 promoted the 'problem-posing' model that Freire spoke about. The psychology underpinning the 1971 Curriculum is as valid today as it was in 1971.[89] Indeed, it has been said that the lack of flexibility on the part of individual teachers and schools in adopting and adapting the 1971 curriculum to meet children's needs could have contributed to some of the school failure and 'drop-out' prevalent throughout the last three decades.[90] S. McAllister Swap, an American researcher, has this in view: 'failing to find a piece of themselves in school, failing to see how past experiences of learning are reflected in school … children may reject or ignore the new information they are receiving and continue to exclusively use their "old" processing schemes'.[91] However, in *Managing Change and Development in Schools*, we are reminded of two fundamental polarities in curriculum. They are the balance or imbalance between individual freedom and social control and the degree of emphasis on the child as a unique individual as distinct from an emphasis on the body of knowledge to be passed on.[92] These polarities need to be off-set one against the other.

The British writer K. Roberts holds that 'Rather than tinkering with the children's presenting culture, maybe we need to devote more effort to making teachers and curricula more responsive to working-class interests'.[93] He holds that the majority of working-class parents have positive attitudes towards schooling and education and that 'if teachers find these attitudes an obstacle rather than a base from which to build, these are grounds for inviting teachers to re-examine their ideas about what constitutes concern, interest, ambition and encouragement'.[94] In his article 'Learning In School and Out', L. Resnik tells us that 'modifying schooling to better enable it to promote skills for learning outside school may simultaneously renew its academic value'.[95] While flexibility and adaptation were key thoughts underpinning the 1971 Curriculum in Ireland these views were rarely defined.

It can be said that schools are expected to offer a broad curriculum suitable for the development of a range of intelligence,[96] developing a strong self-image in their pupils and the capacity to work individually and as members of a team. According to Widlake 'schools urgently need to consider ways and means of shedding their image as being inimical to styles and contents of learning other than the "academic" or the purely functional (i.e. training youngsters to be "followers" as opposed to "leaders")'.[97] Writing about *Taking Student Responsibility Seriously,* D. Ericson and F. Elleth speak of the leadership role of the 'student' as one of 'responsibility' for their own learning but add that this 'does not eliminate the very real responsibilities shared by parents, educators, the state and society at large'.[98]

This broad approach calls for a radical change on the part of the school as a unit[99] and on the part of the school as a unit and the families as a group.[100] It must examine the relationship between a specific teacher and a specific child 'since the face and voice of the teacher can confirm their domination or can reflect enabling possibilities'.[101] It must focus the role of an individual teacher and an individual parent 'we are organised to share with each other what we know about our children's education...[and] educational issues'.[102] A broad approach calls on the school and other agencies with an educational role in the community[103] to work together, providing an integrated service to marginalised children and their families. Radical change is called for from representatives of parents and teachers and local community involved in the decision-making process on educational issues. The outcome of this radical change, which has 'come to be called the "educative community" – that totality of experiences which the child assembles from home, environment, and peer-group – so forcefully dictates how or whether a child will respond to educational stimuli that teachers ignore it at their peril'.[104]

Schools are called on to develop attitudes and behaviours that will lead to individual and team growth 'where the staff is optimally secure, energised, motivated and able to meet their psychological, social and intellectual needs,'[105] and are 'cohesive enough to be willing to buy some shared set of goals'.[106] In an American study the researchers found that shared beliefs and values, collegiality of teachers, their taking on an extended role can actively help 'at risk' students to overcome impediments 'to school membership and academic engagement'.[107]

Studies have found that when teachers had a strong wish to develop 'schools as communities of support for students and teachers' their perceptions of classroom disorder were significantly lower, as was teacher absenteeism.[108] A Californian study noted that pupils found school 'neither discouraging nor motivating, or satisfying ... Most struggled reluctantly ... in a school system that has been accused of being discouraged with itself and of projecting low expectations from most of its students'.[109] In similar observations in Boston, a researcher stated that she 'encountered no consistent expectation among teachers ... that all children could be successful in school'.[110] In *Holding At-Risk Students: The Secret is One-on-One* the author believes that improving students perceptions of the degree of concern that teachers feel for them would positively affect students' attitudes about school and increase the likelihood of their staying on to graduate'.[111]

There have been demands for in-career development for teachers so that they may use their 'expertise as managers of learning and arrangers of learning opportunities'.[112] To learn about professional practice and 'to develop as professional educators requires that we engage in the making of new forms, new relations and connections and by continually transforming what we know'.[113] Success for all children it is argued, depends on attitudes and, in particular, on the possibilities within education. It calls for a 'new professionalism among all those whose work takes them into the field'.[114] Similar sentiments are postulated by Widlake when he defines a professional as one with 'capacity for systematic change ... capacity to adapt and redefine their own expertise ... an ability to convince others that their expertise is genuine, useful and relevant'.[115] We can say that 'teacher, student and parent motivation is one of the single most important questions we face ... a multi-faceted issue touching many dimensions of education'.[116]

For too long the role of education rested with schools. Parents have been traditionally viewed and dealt with as clients, 'dependent on experts' opinions ... passive in the receipt of services ... apparently in need of redirection ... peripheral to decision making ... perceived as "inadequate" and "deficient"'.[117] In addition the child and/or the family was seen as the object of education. An alternative position is that education is only valid when one works 'with' and not 'for', when individuals reach the 'conviction as subjects, not as objects'.[118] Hence the advice of Wolfendale that 'education, in its formal sense, or learning, to use its widest sense, becomes, therefore, too important and vital a commodity to be left to schools'.[119]

Children's Learning

Research has clearly revealed that parental involvement in their children's learning enhances their educational opportunities. The home has been identified as a primary learning environment that is facilitated through the attachment process. When children enter school they bring with them their 'cultural mapping' and when family culture and/or social class differs from that of the school we have seen that 'conflicts may arise for the children in their academic and social adjustment'.[120]

R. M. Clark, an American whose area of interest was family life and school achievement, studied ten black high school students and their families. His views are as follows:

> Families that incorporated frequent dialogue between parents and children and were warm and supportive towards their children, yet set clear and consistent limits, had students who were high achievers. The fact that these families were also single-parent families, of low socio-economic or educational levels, was not significant. The parents of successful students held common attitudes towards the importance of education.[121]

However, working-class children can face obstacles en route to success as 'few working-class children have parents and relatives capable of offering advice and information that middle class homes can furnish on how to manipulate the educational system'.[122] The advantages for children whose parents have had lengthy exposure to second- and third-level education are outlined by Lynch in Chapter One.

Working-class parents are just as likely as the middle classes to see education as a means of advancement and to value it for this reason but 'the longer-term life-chances of working-class pupils have not improved commensurately because levels of attainment among the middle classes have also risen, keeping them as far ahead as ever'.[123] There is little reason for parents' councils, dominated by the middle classes, to upset patterns being reproduced in schools as their children are 'the prime beneficiaries of the system'.[124] The way ahead would seem to lie in enhancing the ability of working-class communities, especially working-class homes, to support children educationally. The success of the middle-class school lies in the fact that the language, the values and the aspirations in the catchment area are more appropriate for schooling, as presently defined, than in the working-class school. Schooling is presently dominated by middle-class values and controlled by middle and upper class decision-makers. 'A solution would entail alterations on both sides in making schooling more apposite for the subculture in question and in drawing parents more readily into the actual educational process'.[125] Strong links between school and community enhance educational outcomes.[126]

Creative teaching and student motivation are two basic elements of the learning process. They are not independent factors that students and teachers bring to the educational process. As Seeley would claim, they are 'the products of a relationship – a productive learning relationship between students and teachers and between home and school'.[127] He claims that the voice of those in education must be heard 'in classrooms and schools, in parent-teacher conferences and in one-on-one discussion between teachers and students'.[128] A different point of view is postulated by middle-class mothers in the *Journal of Curriculum Studies*: 'school experience should be academic and can't deal with social problems ... teachers are wasting their time asking children what they think about things rather than giving them information'.[129] P. Block who has been at the centre of changing organisations, including schools, for the past twenty-five years advocates a partnership that is willing 'to give more choice to the people we choose to serve. Not total control, just something more equal'.[130]

Three British lecturers in Education express anxiety at the unproved claims made by teachers of parental attitudes 'uninterested parents' those who 'want to take over' and the view that 'you never see the parents that you really want to see'.[131] A further cause for concern was the fact that parents as a valuable resource were 'seldom even recognised by schools and teachers, let alone productively tapped'.[132] With the foregoing in mind it is no wonder that Wolfendale's view of schools is that they 'are an insufficient provider of what only the community *in toto* should be offering towards the fullest development and educational opportunity of every child ... and cannot contribute maximally ... without recourse to children's caretakers and without the incorporation of the wider community network'.[133]

Wolfendale encapsulates much modern thought in this quotation. The physical, mental, moral, social, cultural and religious development of the young person cannot be achieved in isolation. The interrelatedness of home, community and school is vital to the all-round development of the young

person. In addition, neither parents, teachers, nor community
agents can achieve with the young person alone. The literature
refers to this as 'contextual' child development.[134] Wolfendale's
quotation serves as a summary statement on home-
community-school based learning and as a lead in to examples
of good practice.

Parents and Education in Selected Countries

When we come to look at the actual situation and educational
practice it is easy to state generalities. Just as Americans are all
said to be in favour of 'motherhood and apple pie' so all
educationalists will see possible roles for parents, teachers and
pupils. However, the concrete expression of values varies from
place to place. A number of initiatives in Britain and America
will be referred to while two initiatives, one in Trinidad and
Tobago and the second in Israel, will be covered in some depth.

Passing quickly over the obvious generalisations, one can
indicate some matters of particular interest. Firstly, some areas
of interest in Britain are identified. In Coventry findings include
many similarities between work practices there and the HSCL
Scheme in Ireland.[135] An interesting fact is that community
education has a 'permanent place' within the education service.
Home-school relationships are a priority. The schools achieve
high levels in oral and written languages and in reading
comprehension.[136] Nottingham promotes an interlink of policy
and practice.[137] Home/school relations are viewed as a
responsibility for all schools, and opportunities are developed to
provide mutual support.[138] The model of partnership found in
Pen Green Nursery in Corby, Northamptonshire[139] – listening to
parents, identification of their needs, networking and the
involvement of parents with their children and in policy-
making resembles practices in Early Start[140] and the HSCL
Scheme in Ireland. A school in Reading[141] is notable for the
simplicity and the practicality of its practices with parents.

Among them were the welcoming of parents, listening to parents, helping parents to prepare children for school, curriculum support and home visitation. Outcomes for children included the valuing of autonomy and choice for children and providing for their emotional needs and their protection. Care of the withdrawn and vulnerable child was also a priority. In Reading there is a very strong sense of the school as community. Outcomes for children included extra support in reading and mathematics with improved performance and a higher level of enthusiasm. Out-of-school activities became a priority as was the issue of multi-racial education.

The key to academic success in the New Haven schools[142] stemmed from the bonding of children with the schools through personal development. For staff the development was that of coping with change. Comer focused on the development of learning by building supportive bonds between children, parents and school. Comer believed that the child's experiences at home coloured their performance in school. There were serious attendance needs and problems with indiscipline. In fact, he held that there was a 'misalignment between home and school'. With parents and staff, Comer and his team focused on problem-solving rather than on blaming. Results indicated that social performance and learning significantly improved, there was increased staff motivation and students in the fourth grade had reached the national norm within a few years.

In Boston and New York the Schools Reaching Out programme provided support for families, particularly the marginalised. Many activities brought parents and teachers closer.[143] However, due to the brevity of the programme the parent-teacher relationship was not developed beyond the point of teachers wanting the home to adapt to the needs of the school while parents wanted the school to adapt to the needs of the home. In Boston and New York parents were viewed as 'useful and important in accomplishing the school's objectives' when barriers were broken down.[144]

The Bernard van Leer Foundation

Bernard van Leer, a Dutch industrialist, supported a broad range of humanitarian causes. In 1949 he created the Bernard van Leer Foundation, (BvLF), to channel his money to charitable purposes after his death (1958). Under the leadership of his son Oscar van Leer (1914-1996), the Foundation started to focus on enhancing opportunities for children and young people who were growing up in circumstances of social and economic disadvantage in order to develop their innate potential. This very important work is carried out on a world-wide basis.

The Foundation accomplishes its objectives through two interconnected strategies. Firstly, by assisting the development of contextually appropriate approaches to childhood care and development through grant aid. Secondly, by disseminating the wealth of knowledge and experience that is generated by projects in order to inform and influence policy. The information is spread through quality publications and videos. For the purposes of this study we shall outline the work done by Pantin, Paz and Salach in projects funded by the Bernard van Leer Foundation, where an essential ingredient of projects is the close involvement of parents and community. This involvement builds up local skills and self-image, so that an entirely new dimension is introduced into the context of the school. The Foundation stresses familiarity with the wider community and its reality and the importance of real life experiences, so that professional services may be transformed.[145] The Bernard van Leer Foundation co-funded the work of G. Pantin in Trinidad and Tobago and of R. Paz and S. Salach in Israel. Paz reminds us that 'communities are untapped reservoirs of human potential'.[146] The Foundation also noted that when parents are interested, community members are brought together, 'children learn how to communicate better together' and 'adult mothers…can group around their shared interest in the child'.[147] The work of the Bernard van Leer Foundation through Pantin, Paz, and Salach has been chosen here because of the strong parallels between their programmes and the HSCL Scheme in Ireland.

Trinidad and Tobago

One of the most interesting community and education projects funded by the BvLF is the 'Servol' one in Trinidad and Tobago. 'Servol' (Service Volunteered For All) operates out of the Port of Spain and its activities cover much of the two-island Republic of Trinidad and Tobago. The population is 1,253,000 with just 50,300 on Tobago and the rest on Trinidad, which has one of the most ethnically diverse populations in the Caribbean.[148]

Servol started in 1970 in Trinidad. As a consequence of civil disorder the area was inhabited by people who were 'poorly educated and poorly housed, had little chance of finding or holding down a job, and who believed that their ability to succeed in life was virtually nil. A major problem was the lack of a stable family life'.[149] The Project Director, Pantin, went from street-corner to street-corner, speaking to groups, while the people 'watched and weighed the situation they wanted so much to believe … they were all desperately in need of help … but suppose it was just another scheme … could they bear the burden of yet another disappointment?'[150] Pantin never offered to give anything to an individual or to a group, rather, he made a deal to share the cost and the effort. Servol is not a welfare organisation. It does not give handouts. Respectful intervention also means respect for the other's dignity 'those who receive also give and those who give receive much'.[151]

As already stated, Trinidad and Tobago were chosen because of the strong similarity in theory and practice with the HSCL Scheme in Ireland. In Trinidad and Tobago Pantin developed his theories of 'Attentive Listening', 'Respectful Intervention', 'Cultural Arrogance' and 'The Philosophy of Ignorance' all emanating from a simple question, 'how can I help you?' Thus he advises 'You listen to the people … you never stop listening … you begin to hear the voice of the people as the important element of their own development…you let the thing grow in its own way and in its own time'.[152] Pantin elaborates further on this theory in *A Mole Cricket Called Servol*. He advises that the community workers must take cognisance of the attitudes, values and priorities of the local people. In addition, the community workers must present their views for discussion, in the realisation that the local people have the choice of accepting or rejecting them.[153]

Pantin believes that this process 'hurts' the community worker, for some time, but it actually spurs them on to a respectful understanding of the people, thus enabling the local community 'to follow the road they have chosen and not the one you feel they should travel'.[154]

By 1975, Servol had many courses for young people in skills as varied as welding, music, plumbing, painting, carpentry and childcare. In order to unite activities Servol started building the Beetham centre and 'in typical Servol fashion, the construction was undertaken almost entirely by its own trainees'.[155] This building became the first Servol 'Life' centre and was opened in 1978, the word 'Life' being added at this stage. Activities included training in a number of vocational skills.

The Life Centre became the focus for a unique course now known as the Adolescent Development Programme (ADP). The interesting feature of courses in the Life Centre is that they ranged from skills development through to parenting skills for teenagers. Pantin outlined the Centre's work in building boy-girl relationships that were not based on sexual exploitation, in non-threatening relationships with an adult, in a relationship of respect with senior citizens and in self-understanding and personal development. He added that all the time the skill training continued, the rebuilding of family life was seen as a real challenge.[156]

What is surely impressive is that the group he was working with was two hundred boys and girls between the ages of fifteen and nineteen, with one or no functioning parent, so that they were drop-outs from school, carrying knives and addicted to marijuana. He saw them as a rootless, disadvantaged group of young people, brutalised by life-experience and their environment. Each Community and Regional Life Centre is different 'reflecting the area where it is located, the background of the trainees, and also the interests and personalities of the staff'.[157]

Very young children have been the heart of Servol from the beginning, from its early attempts to help communities to set up their own pre-schools and to train young women from the communities to run them. Servol has evolved a pre-school teacher training programme. This course is based at the Caribbean Life Centre and the Port of Spain and consists of one year full-time study and two years internship. This programme is accredited by the University of Oxford in England, following a refusal from the University in West Indies due to entry requirements. The training programme is based on child development and teaching methods with major emphasis on parental and community involvement. 'It is not unusual for parents to help out in the classroom, in many cases they will even take over ... they assist with field trips ... they are occasions for teachers, children, parents to get to know one another ... they provide opportunities for outings which very few families can afford by themselves and they are a learning experience for all concerned'.[158]

Pantin sought to bring families together, and to overcome 'broken promises, disillusionment and exploitation'.[159] Speaking about nursery schools, Pantin quotes a researcher with approval, 'the nursery school becomes a sort of listening device through which you can listen attentively ... intervene respectfully ... they play an integral part in both planning and implementation ... it prevents you from making a lot of mistakes'.[160]

The Government of Trinidad and Tobago asked Servol to co-operate in the dissemination of its two major programmes, for adolescents and in pre-schools, throughout the country. This led to a major policy shift and by September 1990 thirty-one Life Centres for adolescents and one hundred and fifty-five pre-schools had been established. All these facilities were run under the auspices of the joint Ministry of Education/Servol Programmes and were locally managed by Boards of Education made up of local community members. The former Ministry of Education Pre-School Unit was disbanded. In addition to education services Servol has been involved in agriculture, fisheries, medical services, adult education, local community development and in small business enterprises. All the programmes emerged as a response to a need, both expressed and underlying, of the people it had been working 'with'. Addressing the expressed needs enabled Pantin and his co-workers to address the underlying needs. They did not solve the poverty issues of Trinidad and Tobago, the problems of family life in inadequate housing or unemployment, but they did 'motivate people...people are beginning to believe in themselves'.[161]

As an outcome, it can be said that the agenda of Servol is being fulfilled in many ways, firstly, by insisting that centres are run by communities. Secondly, the adolescent programmes deal with actual and potential parents at an age when they are still open to new ideas. Next, the pre-school teacher training programme emphasises the role of parents in bringing up their children above the role of the teacher. Fourthly, parents are expected to play a role in the adolescent programmes as well. Pantin sees 'parenting and self-awareness as the crucial parts of the programme, because these help to train people to be parents in a more enlightened way and, ultimately, this will transform society'.[162]

The illustrations we have been citing show the 'partner' concept as including parents being active and central in decision-making and implementation, contributing to, as well as receiving, services. They are recognised as having equal strengths and equivalent expertise, and are mutually accountable with professionals.

Israel

As already stated, the work of Paz and Salach has also been included because of the strong similarities in policy and practice with the HSCL Scheme in Ireland. Paz worked in Ofakim and Negev in Israel. Salach adapted and implemented, in so far as this is possible using a community development process, the policies of Paz in Israel. Early programmes aimed at disadvantaged communities generally focused on children in isolation from their families and environment and were based on the notion of compensation for deficits. In this book, Chapter Two, Chapter Three and part of Chapter Four hold the central argument that in the HSCL Scheme and similar schemes life chances of children can be enhanced by improvements in their surroundings.

When the report of the Prime Minister's Commission for Children and Youth in Distress was published in 1973 it shocked Israel by its revelation of the extent of educational and social disadvantage. In 1974 Paz became involved in a volunteer project in Ofakim, in northern Negev. This project, in its initial phase, seemed 'over-directive' and 'paternalistic', creating another form of 'dependants'.[163] Following discussion with the mayor of Ofakim, a project proposal was submitted to the Bernard van Leer Foundation. The submission sought a community-delivered integrated programme.[164] In September 1977, the Foundation approved the proposal.

Ofakim had a population of eleven and a half thousand and there was a high birth rate. Skilled jobs were scarce and unemployment was high among young people. Most of the professional jobs were held by commuters.

The community in Ofakim was asked to define its needs, establish priorities and develop its resources. Two primary schools were chosen for a community school programme 'to encourage parent participation in the life of the school and the school involvement in the life of the community'.[165] Involvement by parents in a network of kindergartens was also established. The project experienced difficulties and fears of extinction because of political issues. Para-professionals were trained in this project as they were in Morasha with Salach. In both projects, emphasis was placed on the training of local people to continue on their own 'to move from being passive and dependent recipients of assistance ... to becoming active members of the community able to give to others'.[166]

During the first three years of the project the emphasis had been on intervention and the plan for the next phase was that of consolidation. During the project's second three-year phase, a third neighbourhood centre was opened and programmes for teenage girls were initiated jointly with the Department of Welfare. The parent programmes in the kindergartens provided the impetus for another programme developed in conjunction with the Ministry of Education and the Early

Childhood Resource and Training Centre. In the neighbourhood family centres, mothers' and toddlers' groups evolved into play groups. Morning activity sessions were designed and implemented by the para-professionals and the mothers.

In December 1982, the Bernard van Leer Foundation terminated funding and by the end of 1983, with politics favourable towards the project, it was transferred to the municipality. Ofakim Community Centre was assigned the administration and co-ordination of the project's activities preserving its integrated character. The Community Centre fell victim to power struggles. Directors with little understanding of the project rationale came and went. Projects were terminated as funding ceased.[167] The outcomes according to Paz are that 'concerted and coordinated efforts did indeed change parents' perceptions of their role in the education of their children ... innovations became a permanent feature of community life, such as enrichment centres, the parents' cooperative playgroup, and the Early Childhood Research Centre'.[168]

The integrated community education programme did not act as a lever for social change, according to Paz, and she is 'by no means sure' that the quality of life was 'significantly improved' in this 'backwater of a town'.[169] However, Ofakim provided a model for other initiatives and 'the indigenous para-professional came to be regarded as the mainstay of community education'.[170] In Morasha the women who began the Early Childhood and Family Project are 'successfully running family day care centres in their home, some work as para-professional counsellors in other communities, others are continuing their studies in institutions of higher education.'[171]

Perhaps the experience of Paz has enabled Salach to provide more opportunity for interdependent functioning when funding was withdrawn. However, Salach also regrets that the 'reality is still far from the vision of an autonomous community'.[172]

It seems that the Bernard van Leer Foundation and the local agents withdrew funding in both these cases in Israel prematurely. Both projects still required 'nurturing at the community level' when they were asked to stand alone.[173] Both project leaders, Paz and Salach regret that they did not 'manage within the project to deal more intensively and deeply with the ability of the community to take over the work and carry it on'.[174] This would entail keeping the delegation process clearly in focus from the very early stages of programme development.

Summary of Key Issues: Views of Educators and Models of Practice

If schools are to be places of learning within the home-community context, where learning should be on-going, then parents and teachers must be helped to self-confidence. Legal rights, the task of governments to provide for education, good habits of consultation and communication on education policies and skills development all lead to establishing this confidence. The countries examined displayed some of the features, while no one country displayed all the features.

In this chapter we have reviewed some of the work of educators relating to the involvement of the home, the community and the school in children's learning. We began with an acknowledgement of the rights of parents and worked through home-based learning, community-based learning and school-based learning, culminating in a summary on children's learning. Home, community and school were viewed both separately and as interdependent and are inherently integrated. Finally, practices in Britain and America were named while Trinidad and Tobago and Israel were given in some detail. The rationale for this choice was the parallel between them and the HSCL Scheme in Ireland.

The work of Pantin in Trinidad and Tobago has coloured the development of the HSCL Scheme in Ireland. We draw particular attention to his theories of 'Attentive Listening', 'Cultural Arrogance' and 'The Philosophy of Ignorance'. Servol provided many life skills courses: welding, music, plumbing, painting, child care and carpentry. Life centres were opened and included training in a number of vocational skills. Parenting skills were developed with teenagers and care was given to the 'rebuilding of family life'. The approach was 'preventative' because of its work with the very young child.

From the experience in Israel we note that the learning for Paz and Salach was to allow the local community to become autonomous. This is a valuable contribution to developing communities and was initially achieved through intervention, through a consolidation phase to successfully running programmes and acting as para-professionals.

There is a strong awareness among educators of the need to enable parents and teachers to work collaboratively in the development of the whole-child. There is an emphasis on the development of parents and local community particularly in areas of socio-economic disadvantage. That same emphasis needs to be placed on the development of teacher attitudes and behaviour so that the school becomes a community resource. In the next chapter we shall examine the philosophy and structures of the HSCL Scheme in Ireland.

CHAPTER THREE

Focus Points: Teacher, Parent, Pupil

IT HAS ALREADY been stated that under-achievement in school, unsatisfactory retention rates and poor participation in higher education have long been linked to the absence of a favourable home and community environment particularly in areas of identifiable socio-economic disadvantage. Consequently, successive Irish Ministers for Education and the Department of Education had undertaken various initiatives over the years to alleviate the effects of disadvantage on children's education. In 1984, a scheme of special funding for schools in designated areas of disadvantage was initiated.

There is a particular difficulty in writing about the Home/School/Community Liaison Scheme (HSCL) in Ireland. Unlike schemes in other countries and unlike many educational initiatives in Ireland in the past forty years, there has been little primary research, excluding the Rutland Street Project,[1] in the area of home and school.

The HSCL Scheme has evolved through activities, trial and error, planning, implementing, and evaluating within the Department of Education over an eleven year period. The author has been involved in this process at every stage. The problem, therefore, of exploring the HSCL Scheme in Ireland is the lack of records in journals, newsletters and correspondence to which reference might be made. A second difficulty is the fact that a full evaluation will not be possible for some time yet as the scheme is on-going and has very long-term goals. A first evaluation of the HSCL Scheme was completed in 1994.[2] A further evaluation of the practical and theoretical issues that are at work in the scheme was completed in 1999.[3]

There is, however, a real advantage in the present author presenting an outline of the HSCL Scheme. This exposition has the strength and weaknesses of an insider's view. The most obvious weakness that one might fear would be prejudice, unbalanced evaluation arising from being too close physically, temporally and, one might add, emotionally, through the evolution of the scheme. The alert reader will be aware of this weakness and the risks involved. A positive value lies precisely in it being an insider's view. The reader can have some idea of what those in the Department of Education were trying to achieve, how they saw the scheme, the management theories, values, strategies, and philosophy used and underlying the work. With these few clarifications we can attempt a description and some evaluation of the history of the HSCL Scheme.

The aim of this Chapter is to outline the reason why the Department of Education in Ireland established HSCL. A further aim is to clarify the purpose, the preparation made, the processes used and the outcomes noted from activities and initiatives at local school level so that the reader can have an overall picture of the scheme in Ireland.

Historical Background

In 1990, the Minister for Education, Mary O'Rourke, launched a major initiative in HSCL with a pilot scheme involving the appointment of thirty teachers as liaison coordinators in fifty-five primary schools. These local coordinators were appointed from the staff of one of the schools that they served to work on a full-time basis with adults in the home-community and school setting. In-career development for coordinators, was a priority with the Department of Education from 1990. The three-year pilot phase of the scheme ended in June 1993. At the end of the pilot stage the HSCL Scheme became a mainstream resource at primary and post-primary levels. All designated disadvantaged primary and post-primary schools were offered a liaison service from September 1999. The HSCL Scheme has received unstinting support from the various Ministers for Education, Senior Inspectors and civil servants from its initiation to date.

In 1991 the Minister for Education issued a circular[4] to all primary and post-primary schools. The circular 'Parents as Partners in Education' urged that policies be formulated and practice in partnership be initiated nation-wide. The resource personnel and finance were allocated to designated areas of disadvantage.

The Theoretical Evolution of the HSCL Scheme

The HSCL Scheme has evolved both theoretically and practically over the years. Theory has informed practice and practice in turn has informed the theory. With regard to the theory or philosophy of the HSCL Scheme there are several important stages. The first stage was the creation of 'Aims'[5] which were worked out in the Department of Education during the Summer of 1990. The second stage soon followed, which involved the development of twelve 'Basic Principles'[6] devised within the Department of Education in 1990. These principles controlled the evolution of the scheme from 1990-1993. There was little modification in their formulation when finally they were published for schools in 1993. An examination of the Aims and Principles highlights the philosophy and points to significant stages in the practical development of the scheme.

Philosophy of the HSCL Scheme

Aims for the HSCL Scheme were worked out by Dep
of Education personnel during the summer of 1990. \ ...ve
Aims of the HSCL Scheme focus on the 'at risk' pupil,
promoting cooperation between home, school and community,
empowering parents, retaining young people in the education
system and disseminating good practice. Extensive discussion
and study took place within the Department of Education. As
the work of developing the scheme was an on-going process
involving formal and informal discussion within the
Department and with others, it is not possible or even desirable
to attempt to indicate the source of the various ideas that came
together to form Aims and Basic Principles of the HSCL
Scheme. We were aware of various educational writing,
especially Pantin and the work of the Bernard van Leer
Foundation, though we may not always have been conscious of
direct borrowing. More significant perhaps was the cumulative
experience of the group, as well as shared vision based partly
on educational convictions and partly on practical experiences
in the field. The implementation of these aims has remained a
priority for the management of the HSCL Scheme since its
initiation in November 1990.

The underlying philosophy of the HSCL Scheme is one that
seeks to promote partnership between parents and teachers.
The purpose of this partnership is to enhance the pupils'
learning opportunities and to promote their retention within
the educational system. This is pursued by identifying and
responding to parent needs and by creating a greater awareness
in teachers of the complementary skills of parents / their
children's education. The scheme seeks to promote a
operation between home, school, and relevant co
agencies in the education of young people. The schem
directly on the salient adults in the pupils' education

seeks indirect benefits for the children themselves. In short, the HSCL Scheme seeks to develop the parent as prime educator.

Although presented as a national scheme by the Department of Education, it was always intended that HSCL would be 'area based' and designed at local level with marginalised families in mind. The Department of Education was ready to guide educational change through providing leadership, through pointing out the new direction and through providing the necessary resources, training and support. Believing that self-discovery is the essence of organisational change, the Department's HSCL management team continually endeavoured to bring about change through 'ownership' of the process. This was promoted through a process of individual and group consultations where active listening was advocated and adhered to. It was intended that it should be tailored to meet local needs and that it would flourish through self-generating initiatives.

Modern educators and leaders support this way of thinking. It is interesting to note that in more recent times, a writer who is known for his visionary thoughts and practices when dealing with and implementing change claimed that 'organizational change must be led top-down but must be engineered bottom-up'.[7] The Halton Effective Schools Project held that 'the change process would be 'top-down, bottom-up' – the system would provide broad direction and support for schools' own plans'.[8] While the HSCL Scheme was led 'top-down', the 'bottom-up', area based, approach had been endorsed by the Department of Education since the inception of the scheme in 1990. It was intended that the HSCL Scheme would be developed in each area as a response to local needs but within the framework of the Basic Principles.[9] We shall now elaborate on the twelve Basic Principles underpinning the philosophy and practice of the HSCL Scheme.

The twelve Basic Principles were operative from 1990. Most of them will be virtually self-explanatory. Under each a brief explanation is given, and, where appropriate, practical steps to put these principles into practice are noted. While the Basic Principles existed from 1990, they were not forwarded to schools in written form until 1993. Between 1990 and 1993 the Department of Education allowed practice on the ground to further inform the theory.

The scheme consists of a partnership and collaboration of the complementary skills of parents and teachers
The notion of partnership has been a theme in in-career development for coordinators since the inception of the scheme in 1990. It can be said that schools that operate collaboratively with family and community are much more likely to be effective. Partnership presupposes equality and implies that the relationship has been formed on the basis that each has an equally important contribution to make to the whole. It implies a commitment to working together, exploring possibilities, planning, decision-making and on-going evaluation. An example of this practice is experienced in a well functioning Local Committee.[10] Partnership as a way of working is challenging and calls for changes in individual and corporate attitudes, methods of work and structures, particularly on the part of schools. The Department of Education has recognised this and has encouraged whole-school development.

The scheme is unified and integrated at both primary and post-primary levels
The HSCL Scheme began at primary level in 1990 and was extended in 1991 to the post-primary sector. In most school situations a number of coordinators serve the same pupil

catchment area. A junior primary, senior primary and post-primary school campus could have up to three coordinators. It is expected that coordinators use a team approach across the schools, but any one family would deal with only one coordinator. Co-operative activities are provided. One example is the transfer programme for parents and pupils to ease the transition from home to primary school and on to post-primary. In addition, space for parents is shared across the schools in the same catchment areas as are the courses, classes, and activities for parents. It took some time to develop this co-operative approach, which currently varies in quality from area to area.

The thrust of the scheme is preventative rather than curative
The scheme promotes initiatives, which are preventative rather than compensatory or curative. The coordinator works with, and fortifies, the family so that instances of absenteeism and disruption will be obviated. It is the working policy of the Department of Education that engaging home and school in meaningful educational activities promotes the child's interest in school, often reducing absenteeism and disruptive behaviour.

The emphasis on the preventative quality of HSCL work has been difficult to implement because the outcomes are by nature long-term. In their experience of demanding classroom settings, teachers tend to look for short term benefits, and may not be enthusiastic about longer-term remedies. The preventative approach was well expressed at the Community Education Development Centre in Coventry: 'The emphasis should be on habilitation rather than rehabilitation, on self-determined change rather than on the cure of some supposed disease'.[11] The notion of prevention covers such areas as illiteracy, unemployment, drug misuse, jail and psychological collapse.

The focus of the scheme is on the adults whose attitudes and behaviours impinge on the lives of children, namely, parents and teachers

The work with adults enables coordinators to target the needs of both parents and teachers, and indeed those of community personnel also. This principle may perhaps be seen as the kernel of the scheme bringing together and involving as it does, home, school and community. The theoretical justification may again be seen in an English educator who, in identifying favourable learning environments, concludes that just as children need healthy and strong bodies so too do they need 'healthy and strong supporting communities. To that extent, we are in the business of community development, just as much as we are in the business of child development'.[12] The thinking of many other educators was influential in the development of this aspect of the HSCL Scheme.[13] A particular type of in-career development for coordinators, course provision and activities for parents and at times for teachers supported the implementation of the scheme's focus on adults. On other occasions the two groups, parents and teachers, worked together as will be evidenced when we speak later on policy making.

The basis of activities in the scheme is the identification of needs and having those needs met

The focus of the scheme is on the identification of the needs of individuals and families and on the meeting of those needs to enhance the continuity between home, community and school. The theories of an enlightened educator – Pantin – underlie practice here: 'Respectful Intervention', 'Cultural Arrogance', 'The Philosophy of Ignorance'.[14] From the last he advises: 'never presume that you know the needs and priorities of people, confess your utter ignorance of their background, the way their minds work, the reason for their attitudes, and ask them how they would like you to help'.[15]

When the scheme began there was, within the Department of Education and amongst schools, much general awareness of needs, clustering with ideas such as marginalisation, deprivation, 'at risk', disadvantage, unequal opportunity, absenteeism, unruly behaviour, societal and family problems and culture changes. From the initial stages, the Department of Education stressed the fact that the scheme should respond to local needs – 'learning decisions must be made as close as possible to the learning workplace'.[16] The Department encouraged coordinators to focus on parent and teacher attitudes and behaviours so that these key people would work together to develop the whole child. This led to many courses and activities for parents with some in-career development for teachers. In the following years, while this focus was maintained, other needs emerged. An example was the need to focus on the most marginalised.

The development of teacher and staff attitudes in the areas of partnership and the 'whole-school' approach is fostered
Significant clarity has been introduced into the area of teacher/staff/parent relationships through the language of partnership and whole-school. The work involved in developing positive staff attitudes is easy to define, but can be hard to bring about in practice. The scheme demands from professionals new attitudes which challenge their approaches and values. There are three types of in-service provided within the HSCL Scheme – intensive and on-going for coordinators, occasional for principals, and sporadic and by invitation of the school for staff.

The scheme promotes the fostering of self-help and independence
In the second half of the twentieth century the notion of self-help, independence, interdependence and empowerment

became common currency in many disciplines. While all the basic principles of the scheme interlink, there is an obvious bond between the identification and meeting of needs and the fostering of self-help. The Department sought to develop this principle of self-help through training for parents, through encouraging coordinators to identify leadership skills and to delegate as soon as possible to parents. Coordinators have endeavoured to draw together people, actions and events. They have worked with and between groups and programmes. The aim was to encourage people away from dependency and to enable them to make decisions in relation to their own lives and those of their children.[17] The hope of the Department of Education was that when parents change as individuals they will make the transition from personal empowerment to collective growth. This has happened in the case of parents who are now actively involved in their schools. We need to uphold a creative approach to adult learning and community development[18] – individual growth leading to collective advancement.[19]

Home visitation is a crucial element in establishing bonds of trust with families
Home visitation might be seen as a dramatic symbol of the whole scheme. It implies the school going to the home. It demands that those entering the home be respectful and sensitive. Home visitation is open ended in that it is rarely possible to determine in advance the outcome of any single visit or series of visits. Home visitation forms a major part of the role of the coordinators. It is emphasised in the scheme for the purpose of forming bonds of trust and of fortifying all families and pupils in a supportive and self-reliant community. The emphasis on home visitation is particularly directed towards the marginalised. The 'link between understanding the

community and home-visiting is a circular one; much of that local understanding is obtained through talking to parents in their homes'.[20]

Developing parents as home visitors has become a focus in the HSCL Scheme. It is one aspect of their work that coordinators can delegate, a practice promoted by the Department of Education since the inception of the HSCL Scheme. As was recorded in Chapter Two the promotion of the 'para-professional' is often found in the Bernard van Leer Foundation literature. A number of coordinators have adopted this work pattern.

Networking with and promoting the coordination of the work of voluntary and statutory agencies increases effectiveness and obviates duplication

Networking is a consequence of the actual series of relationships and interlocking activities within the community. It challenges many previously held assumptions about job demarcation. From the initiation of the HSCL Scheme the Department of Education placed a lot of emphasis on networking between schools, and of schools with community agencies. In fact, the Department of Education was a pioneer in the area of networking. The language of the Department developed over the years to its current thinking of ensuring an integrated delivery of service to marginalised children and their families. This calls for interdepartmental purpose and interdisciplinary approach to school-based interventions.

In matching needs with services it is anticipated that coordinators initiate the provision of a specific service only when another provider does not already exist. It was felt that networking would heighten awareness of work being done by other agencies and would prevent the duplication and replication of services. The coordinator was expected to use creative, innovative approaches when liaising with personnel already working in local communities.

This Basic Principle, that of networking, is an aspect of the HSCL Scheme that met with resistance initially. The arrival of coordinators – who were teachers – generated a certain fear among other professionals and some voluntary groups. The resistance sprang from the fear that a group of teachers would take over or interfere with other professional and voluntary roles. It took almost three years to quell these fears. The writer is aware of this from both research and observation. Gardaí (Irish police), and public health nurses in all areas and social workers in some areas were both open and responsive. With the on-going support of the Department of Education, literature from the Combat Poverty Agency[21] and the advent of Area Based Partnerships[22] the task became easier.

However, it cannot be denied that networking-integration is a complex and difficult process because of the different expectations people have about what can be achieved and because of the fears already mentioned. Some teachers, moreover, saw networking in a very limited way, namely that of making their teaching role more fruitful or even easier.

Since the Department of Education has expanded its services to schools in designated areas of disadvantage the call for an integrated area-based response to educational disadvantage and to networking is even more formidable.

HSCL is a full-time undertaking
It was realised that HSCL duties could not be added to a teacher's job specification. Firstly, because new responsibilities would create labour relation problems, but more importantly because it was realised that training was needed. It very quickly emerged in the thinking of the Department that the coordinator would have to be not only properly trained, but

also full-time. The Department of Education made it very clear that coordinators could not be deployed to the ordinary day-to-day duties of class or subject teachers. They were additional full-time appointments to the new service, which had been added to the schools in the HSCL Scheme. On the whole, this basic principle does not present difficulties to schools now. In earlier years, however, some schools were very vocal about wanting the coordinator to teach and to carry out routine work such as yard duty, supervision for absent teachers, care for sick children and discipline issues.

The liaison coordinator is an agent of change
As the Department was outlining its Basic Principles it became clear that the key agent of change would have to be properly trained as well as being full-time. Whilst it was recognised that in the partnership model everyone had a contribution to make, the hope for the school in liaison and the focus would have to be on the coordinator. In the light of these Basic Principles there is a special role for the local coordinator as an agent of these changes. To the degree that coordinators have rapport with staff, receive appropriate in-career development and are able to transfer learning, bringing staff with them, they can indeed be agents of change within their area of responsibility.

Perceptions of 'Important Changes' from principals, coordinators and teachers in the 182 schools surveyed by the author[23] are as follows in Table 3.1. There were 362 perceptions relating to the 'most important change'. The changes fell into twenty-two categories, sixteen categories were identified by principals, seventeen by coordinators and twelve by teachers.[24] The twenty-two categories were collapsed and summarised into three categories which were measured against 'helpful/very helpful' and 'unhelpful'. In Table 3.1 which follows we shall find the perceptions of principals, coordinators, and teachers.

Table 3.1 Perceptions of the Most Important Change, According to Principals (P), Coordinators (C), and Teachers (T), and Whether it Was Very Helpful, Helpful, or Unhelpful

Category of Change	Attitude change by school towards parents			Parent enhancement/ participation			School development			Overall satisfaction according to PCT in each category of change		
	%			%	%		%		%			
	P	C	T	P	C	T	P	C	T	P	C	T
Very helpful	67.3	73.9	48.2	67.9	69.6	36.4	33.3	60.0	50.0	66.7	72.3	46.5
Helpful	31.8	26.1	46.4	28.6	30.4	54.5	66.7	40.0	50.0	31.9	27.7	47.9
Unhelpful	0.9	0.0	5.4	3.6	0.0	9.1	0.0	0.0	0.0	1.4	0.0	5.6
Total %	100	100	100	100	100	100	100	100	100	100	100	100
N *(respondents)*	110	115	56	28	23	11	3	10	4	141	148	71

[Percentage rounded up 0.1 per cent in one instance]

From Table 3.1 we note that 'attitude change by the school towards parents' was the most important outcome for principals, coordinators, and teachers. In second place was 'parent enhancement/participation'. These are highly impressive findings on the part of schools as both relate to the parent body. The area of 'school development' just surfaced for principals and teachers (see N) with a more noticeable consideration on the part of coordinators. Holding the wider view, as many coordinators do, they may have visualised the fact of parent involvement as leading to 'school development'.[25] Coordinators did not surface in the 'unhelpful' category of change while some principals and a higher percentage of teachers did surface.

The promotion of community 'ownership' of the scheme is sought through the development of Local Committees
The final principle sought to address the question of ownership. Whilst it was clear that the more people who 'owned' the scheme the better, a serious issue appeared to be how those not professionally involved, as well as teachers, could feel that it was their scheme. The community perspective also needed to be included. It was felt that whereas the school was too narrow a group to take ownership, a group made up of all the parents was too wide and diffuse for the initial sense of ownership. What was chosen was the method of using Local Committees. This wide sense of seeking ownership, it might be remarked in passing, is a reflection of the Department's own experience in having its internal HSCL committee drawn from eleven bodies.[26]

The Local Committee is a vital element in the integrated delivery of service to marginalised children and their families. By its very nature it presupposes an interdisciplinary approach and calls for the inclusion of marginalised but developed parents. The clear thinking of the Department of Education guidelines about Local Committees is evident in correspondence with schools in the early 1990s. It merits mention here. The Local Committees were set up to ensure greater community ownership of the scheme and wider community support for it. Committees would enable parents to have input into the development of the scheme in their own area. It was also envisaged that the Local Committee would help to coordinate the work of various agencies in the area. The Committee members would receive reports from the local coordinator and advise him/her of specific needs. It was anticipated that the Local Committee would support the local coordinator as an important community resource.[27]

The HSCL Scheme can be viewed through organisational and operational structures.

National Steering Committee

The Minister for Education appointed a National Steering Committee (NSC) 'to direct the progress of the pilot project and to advise her'.[28] The NSC had twenty-two members who were representatives of the then Departments of Education, Health and Justice. The parent councils, management bodies and teacher unions at primary and post-primary levels were represented on the NSC, as was the Educational Research Centre and the Economic and Social Research Institute and the then Conference of Major Religious Superiors.

The NSC remained for three years after the pilot phase of HSCL had ended. The role of the NSC was advisory.

National Coordinator

In September 1990, two months before the scheme started, the author was seconded to the Department of Education as National Coordinator of the scheme. For about ten years, as principal of a large urban Dublin primary school, she had been implementing a scheme, which was to become a *de facto* pilot HSCL strategy. The Department of Education was aware, through the local inspector, of the practice of this school. The Department had been planning to introduce a HSCL Scheme. The appointment of the Principal as National Coordinator was intended to promote and extend HSCL practices.

The National Coordinator brought to the appointment the experience of a ten-year principalship, during the 1980s, in an eight-hundred pupil school in a designated area of disadvantage. Throughout these years, HSCL was established and strengthened through the Parents' Room, courses and activities for parents, preparation for and involvement in classroom work and home visitation. This was possible because teachers were taken through a process of preparation, which enabled them to embrace parent partnership with varying degrees of commitment. In a Memorandum for Schools the Department of Education said of this principal 'Over the period of her principalship she has led her staff to the development of a HSCL programme and has developed considerable personal and professional skills'.[29] Linked to the development work with the staff of this school, a teacher was released from classroom teaching to work until midday each day with parent development. In the afternoon, the same teacher worked with colleagues in the classroom developing a coordinated approach towards music in the school.

The Department of Education explained the role of the National Coordinator: 'to advise, support and animate the local coordinators and the local committees. She will liaise with the local coordinators on an individual, local and school cluster basis and will act as a liaison person between the cluster areas and the National Steering Committee'.[30]

Introductory Meeting

When the Department of Education invites a school to become part of the HSCL Scheme, there is an introductory meeting for the chairperson, the principal and a representative staff member from each school. The purpose of the introductory meeting is to disseminate information regarding the aims, basic principles, rationale and practices of the HSCL Scheme. In addition, the meeting offers an opportunity to hear and to work through the expectations, concerns and queries participants might have regarding their involvement in the HSCL Scheme.

The introductory meetings began in 1990, at the inception of the scheme, and continued with each extension to the scheme since. This writer knows from observation that in the early years of these meetings, there was a lot of fear and tension stemming from anxiety around change and the involvement of parents. It is quite different now as issues have been clarified for new schools to the scheme by virtue of the practice on the ground in other schools. It is evident from the progress and from the development of the scheme that the questions now arising are different. In 1993, a further development in the HSCL Scheme took the form of a contract.[31] In 1993, all schools already in the HSCL Scheme and those joining the scheme were required to complete this letter. This was a determined effort to copper-fasten structures and processes in relation to HSCL. When this letter has been returned the selection procedure for the coordinator begins.[32]

In-career Development

As already stated, the HSCL Scheme demands from professionals new attitudes that challenge their approaches and values. The work of the coordinator in strengthening family and community bonds with the school has required the provision of a comprehensive in-career development programme. The programme for coordinators has encompassed personal and professional development, together with leadership and management skills.

It is widely held that effective in-career development sessions should begin with the identification of a need. The gap between the attitudes, knowledge, and skills required for a particular job and the levels currently held by the participants should be part of the consideration. The existence of a training need states that a change is necessary, 'a change from a situation or performance which is below that level required to at least the required level. The change agent is the training event'.[33] Ownership of the training process will evolve if a 'partnership is produced between the three parties, learner, boss and trainer, each contributing their own special expertise'.[34] A similar view holds training as 'a systematic process with some planning and control rather than random learning from experience ... concerned with changing concepts, skills and attitudes ... [improving] effectiveness ... of the organization'.[35] We find here, in synopsis form, four key questions relating to the design of in-career development sessions: are the 'training needs properly identified?' are the 'learning objectives relevant?' are 'performance standards correctly set?' and are the 'right priorities established'.[36]

It can be stated that in-career development training, which was provided through the HSCL Scheme, is linked with all the above findings.

The purpose of in-career development provision is to improve the performance of coordinators so that the effectiveness of the school can be enhanced – 'the purpose of training is not to satisfy the trainer or the training function ... but to provide the learners with the opportunity to improve their *skills for the benefit of the organization*'.[37]

In designing in-career development programmes since September 1990, the in-service planning team constantly viewed and reviewed the expected changes resulting from the in-career development programmes in terms of *individual* performance. In addition it examined how these perceived changes could link into the *effective organisation of the school as a whole*, the principal, staff, parents, Board of Management, Local Committees, and wider community, thus affecting pupil performance. Finally, it perceived how these changes could bring about the overall vision of the HSCL Scheme, that is, to maximise pupil potential.[38]

Methods Used and Skills Developed during In-career Development Sessions

There are three general categories in the delivery of in-career development to coordinators. Firstly there is the *input* of material, secondly comes *interaction* with the facilitator and thirdly, *group* work. Input of material is designed to develop coordinators on a personal and professional level, including skills development. The rationale and current practices of the HSCL Scheme are developed combined with findings from HSCL-type schemes and relevant research evidence internationally. Interaction with the facilitator and among participants takes place regularly to clarify issues and to promote the transfer of learning in the coordinator's home base. Group work blends the needs, expectations and fears that coordinators have with the needs of a developing scheme.

We take a closer look at the skills developed during in-career development sessions. The personal development of coordinators has been concerned with the positive aspects of self-image, decision-making, experience of respect, empowerment and the ability to delegate as positive attributes of the coordinators themselves. It has also been concerned with being models of these qualities and influencing teachers and parents to develop the same skills. Coordinators are also trained and supported so that they can cope with negative feelings and blocks to progress, work to develop positive attitudes and hopefulness in others, and still maintain their energy.

In the skills development area the topics covered included active listening, observation methods, body language, communication, feedback process, trust building and a sense of belonging. Such areas as managing, leading, planning, monitoring and evaluating are among vital elements in the development of any school, and indeed of the HSCL Scheme, and are covered in Chapter Five.

Since coordinators work both within and between groups and on committees the setting up, functioning and characteristics of groups was examined. The reality of belonging to a group, inner circles, group turnover and stages in the development of groups were discussed. Rights and roles with their inherent responsibilities were outlined. An adequate understanding of the cycle of dependence, independence and interdependence within groups was deemed essential, as was the consideration of group defences. Training in the theory and practical aspects of meetings included preparation for meetings, the purpose of meetings, processes used during meetings and the importance of naming outcomes. The conditions necessary for the implementation of outcomes was also considered.

Within the partnership module, aspects covered over the years were the clarification of roles including inherent rights and responsibilities. The rationale of the scheme designed to meet Irish needs was explored. The Basic Principles of the scheme in Ireland were worked through. Experience of partnership from other countries was shared.

Topics and Processes

In relation to general topics, and the processes used, the models of education and their implications were included. So too were processes to identify needs, gifts and differences. The use of structures and evaluation models on an individual and group basis was prominent. Action research involved coordinators reflecting on their practice, reviewing strengths and weaknesses, revising the practice, acting on it and reflecting again on a cyclical basis. The HSCL Scheme encourages the Action Research model. Leadership, including change, attitudes, creativity, empowerment, motivation, delegation, issues around power and the use of power, conflict resolution and oppression were highlighted. The understanding of and the owning of feelings was encouraged. Counselling skills were provided.

Outcomes from In-career Development Sessions

It would appear from talking to school personnel and from research evidence that the foregoing topics, processes and skills development have consequences for schools.[39] The effects for schools, which vary in degree, include the on-going development of the parent as prime educator and the increased effectiveness of coordinators working with principals and the Board of Management. The training of parents as home visitors, facilitators of courses and classes, and deliverers of services with local communities is also in evidence. The continuing growth of cluster groups of coordinators, the setting up of Local Committees, the development of a whole-school approach and a start in the formation of school policy between groups of parents and teachers has taken place. Integration with other Department services to schools in designated areas, namely, Early Start, Support Teacher Project, Breaking the Cycle – urban and rural dimensions, 8-15 Early School Leaver Initiative and the Stay in School Retention Initiative is more obvious. The last two programmes will soon be subsumed into the School Completion Programme. There is an ease in transfer from home to primary school and from primary to the post-primary sector. Networking with voluntary and statutory bodies is much more frequent.[40] However, to be truly effective networking must progress to the integrated delivery of service, at local level, to marginalised children and their families.

The topics covered at in-career development training are given further treatment within the normal HSCL Scheme sequence of review-plan-implement-review. Coordinators need sustained support so that the learning at in-career development sessions does not lose momentum on return to school. The importance of coordinators appropriating this learning cannot be over stressed so that new behavioural attitudes and practices become routine.

The second last phase of the training cycle is the 'incorporation into normal work of new ways of thinking or carrying out tasks'.[41] In a number of schools, coordinators have been actively supported by the principal and management in the transfer of learning. In other situations it was presumed that the coordinator had the motivation and the ability to introduce the HSCL Scheme alone. In order to further facilitate the transfer of learning and the development of the scheme, action plans are a priority during in-career development training. The 'analysis of situations which are likely to test the new learning and the consideration of strategies to enlist support and to deflect opposition' have also been carefully considered through leadership training and conflict resolution modules during in-career development sessions.[42]

The final phase, and yet one that began with the identification of its need, is evaluation. In the HSCL training programme, evaluation runs throughout the process and afterwards into the work place through school visits to coordinators by the National and Assistant National Coordinators where the needs for in-career development training in the future are identified. To expand the process of evaluation more fully it can be stated that there is on-going review with participants during the modules, with opportunities for the group to change the direction. There is an open-ended question validation review at the end of the session. Action planning, which is not specifically an evaluation but a personal contract on the part of the learner, takes place. There is constant evaluation identified through job behaviour and performance at school and community level. Identification of the extent to which the local school community has acknowledged, accepted and promoted the ideals of the HSCL Scheme and the partnership process and the extent to which pupils are staying within the educational system and are benefiting from it is assessed. Evaluation is at all times carried out with people, it is not done for them or to them.

Visits to Schools by the National and Assistant National Coordinators

The National Coordinator and the Assistant National Coordinators visit schools on a regular basis. The main focus when visiting a school is to support the local coordinator. During visits successes are recounted and affirmed, while needs are expressed and discussed. Advice is often sought and followed by shared reflection. There is an opportunity for difficulties to be named and worked through. Realistic goals are considered and aligned with the overall vision of the HSCL Scheme. Monitoring and evaluation techniques are enlisted.

Another important aspect of school visitation is to animate school personnel such as principal, teachers, parents, chairpersons of Boards of Management and members of the wider community. The aim is to encourage and facilitate them to live out the shared vision of partnership in education as defined and exercised in each school community. A visit from the National or Assistant National Coordinators often holds out hope to people who live and work in difficult and demanding conditions. The visits are also a conduit for data gathering. Knowledge gained from first-hand experience of the HSCL Scheme in action at ground level is used to inform and transform the direction of the scheme at national level.

School visits are also an opportunity for networking and for both the encouragement and support of an integrated delivery of service to marginalised young people and their families. Networking has in many instances enhanced respect for the family through more comprehensive services. It has encouraged greater uptake of educational opportunities and has maximised personal resources such as shared thoughts and pooled talents. Networking can establish effective, economical budgetary practices and facilitate time-management. Integrated work should provide an in-built support structure for individuals and groups.

Every effort is made during school visits to involve staff members in the HSCL Scheme. Coordinators are encouraged to focus on this area of work and to discuss ways of involving the principal and staff. This can be achieved through sharing positive current practice about the liaison scheme and through the facilitation of staff sessions regarding the rationale and practice of the scheme. Encouraging in-career development for teachers, helping to raise their self-image and confidence and leading them to work with parents in a more equal partnership is of paramount importance. So too is the supporting of principals in working towards a whole school approach.[43]

Cluster Groups

From the initial stage, clusters of coordinators were established on a regional basis. The Department of Education had given some norms: 'Depending on the demographic structure of the clusters or of areas within clusters, the coordinators will work on an inter-school, local and cluster level and will act as mutually supportive and co-operative teams using their complementary skills to the best advantage'.[44] At this point in time four different types of cluster meeting have developed within the HSCL Scheme.[45]

The Role of the HSCL Coordinator in Ireland

Local Coordinator

We shall now examine the role of the HSCL coordinator as envisaged by the Department of Education. In keeping with the aims and principles of the liaison scheme, the local coordinator must address the development of the parent-teacher relationship and collaboration to enhance the nurturing of the whole child. This implies noting personal and leisure needs, and the curricular and learning needs of parents so as to promote their self-worth and self-confidence. Equally, it implies the development of staff and teacher attitudes and behaviour so that the school becomes a community resource.

Coordinator initiatives are focused on adults, on parents and teachers, rather than on children, but should impinge – indirectly and over time – on children's lives. The initiatives are concerned with promoting parents' education, development, growth and involvement. The participation of parents in their children's education, including homework support, is encouraged. A parents' room is provided, as are crèche facilities for parents who attend programmes in the school. Of particular importance is the developing of principal and teacher attitudes towards partnership and a whole-school approach. Parents and teachers are encouraged to collaborate, sharing their complementary skills, experiences and knowledge.

Almost all initiatives, including courses and classes for parents, were organised as a direct result of a needs identification process held by the coordinators on both a formal and an informal basis. Examples of HSCL Scheme activities for parents, organised by coordinators, can be categorised on four broad levels. There tends to be a pattern in the participation-involvement of parents. Some parents progress through a sequence, while others enter at a particular stage. Leisure time activities are a non-threatening starting point for marginalised parents. This is often followed by curricular activities so that parents may come closer to their children's learning. Personal development courses including parenting, leadership skills development, and involvement in formal learning seem to come in third place. Lastly, we note parents supporting and becoming a resource to their own children, to coordinators and to teachers by organising activities. These parents pass on their skills to children by acting as teacher aides in the classroom and as support persons in the community.[46]

It is held by the Department of Education that activities are never viewed as ends in themselves, but rather as a means of enabling parents to fulfil their role as primary educators of their children, thus encouraging maximum benefit from the school system and retention in it. Parents are also encouraged to make decisions in relation to their own lives and those of their children. Activities included home maintenance, cookery, art and craft, money management, parents' choir, gardening, helping with the school environment and dancing. Parenting took place at an informal level through all the school activities, which in many instances led to formal parenting programmes. Curricular development generally centred around basic mathematics, Irish, English and computers in order to enable parents to help their own children. For senior primary and post-primary pupils parents got involved in study-skills procedures so that they could support their children's homework practice.

In the areas of personal development and formal learning, programmes in parenting, substance awareness, leadership and child care training and child protection programmes were included. Self-development programmes to raise self-worth and self-confidence were popular with parents. Courses on facilitation skills for parents were sought. Pre-entry classes for parents on language, numeracy, nutrition and social skills helped parents to support their children's learning. Toy libraries were established. Transfer programmes were the focus of meetings organised jointly by primary and post-primary coordinators for parents of pre-entry pupils, sixth class pupils, their parents and their teachers. It should be noted that formal learning spanning the spectrum from basic literacy to the Leaving Certificate has taken place within the HSCL Scheme.

Parents are a resource to their own children and also to the wider school community. As we have already noted, various programmes in schools, ranging from pre-entry through to Leaving Certificate level, enable parents to help and support their children's learning. Parents work with children in the classroom in such areas as reading/paired reading, art and craft activities, drama, library organisation, mathematics, computers and cookery. At post-primary level parents work with young people in the classroom on topics such as peer pressure, and the prevention of substance misuse and teenage pregnancy. A number of parents deliver modules to pupils doing the Leaving Certificate Applied[47] in areas such as interviewing technique and relationships in the work place. In addition to helping their own children with homework, many parents are involved, on a rota basis, in community run 'homework clubs' where children who have personal or home difficulties around homework are encouraged, helped and supported.[48] This branches out to include third level students who give their time and support on a voluntary basis. One college of education has students involved in pairs with Leaving Certificate pupils who have had babies. One student teacher helps the young mother with her homework while the other student teacher cares for the baby. In another situation, the young mothers come to the school on Saturday morning with their babies who are cared for in the crèche while their mothers are involved in personal development and parenting programmes. All these efforts are intended to support the young mother in parenting and to enable her to remain in education.

Other features of the role of the coordinator involved setting up a parents' room and crèche facilities. When difficulties arose, where perhaps a group of parents was dominant in the room, most coordinators have successfully facilitated a process to remedy this. The parents' room provided a forum for a non-verbal method of communication and is one of the strongest ways of making parents feel comfortable and welcome in the school.

The role of the coordinator also includes a systematic approach to home visitation. Home visitation is a purposeful outreach dimension of the HSCL Scheme to parents. It is both a symbolic and a real expression of interest in families, many of which have been alienated from the educational system in the past. So the purpose of home visitation is clear. During the visits, coordinators give information and they support parents in the education of their children and seek to establish a rapport with the parents. Coordinators offer information about the services available in the community. They encourage parents to become involved with the community, to work with community needs and to harness community energy thereby enabling the community to solve its own problems. Through home visits the coordinators endeavour to show the welcoming, hopeful and human face of the school in the context and circumstances of daily life. Coordinators also seek out potential parent leaders who are willing to participate in the HSCL Scheme's activities and to share their talents. These parents are directed towards relevant training. Coordinators aim at helping parents to express their fears around approaching schools. They seek to break down negative attitudes among parents towards schools and schooling.

It is highly recommended by the Department of Education that home visitation be carried out in a caring way. Coordinators are expected to be sensitive to the needs of the person. Coordinators aim to be non-threatening and friendly and they work with the family agenda. Coordinators try to show a willingness to listen and to stay as long as is necessary. Coordinators state that the quality of the contact far outweighs the relevance of quantity where home visits are involved.[49]

Encouragement is the key word in home visitation. There is a deep awareness that one is there for the good of the family – coordinators offer support and gently encourage parents into the school.

Regarding outcomes from home visitation, coordinators state that being involved in visits is a learning experience where they get an insight into the real needs, fears, successes, frustration and interests of parents. Coordinators say parents are 'impressed' that they 'care enough to call'. Listening to parents' needs strengthens bonds of trust and parents feel valued. As a result many parents have joined in school activities.

Parents as Community Leaders and as Educational Home Visitors

Some parents with basic training volunteered to participate in advanced training for parents. Parents selected became deeply involved in the community. A group of parents and coordinators monitor this process at local level. Parents have, for some time, facilitated parenting and personal development programmes for other parents.

A further and exciting development is the training of parents as educational home visitors. This practice embodies the principle of delegation, of parents in the role of multiplier, and affords more opportunity to reach the most marginalised families. Parents who have been empowered and affirmed now have the capacity to visit other families and to offer support. Each home visitor is equipped with a relevant information pack for the primary and/or the post-primary school. These packs contain information about school activities, uniform, book rental scheme, policies on homework, punctuality, school transfer and good behaviour. Home visitors often listen to the expectations and concerns of parents particularly in relation to the transfer to post-primary school. A number of the home visitors are involved in pre-reading/reading and storytelling in the local health centre, again on a voluntary basis, with young children awaiting their turn to attend the doctor.

Parents are also a resource in some of the supervised study centres or 'homework clubs' organised by coordinators for marginalised families and funded through the Area Based Partnership.[50] The 'core group' of involved parents who are close to the coordinator and to the activities of the HSCL Scheme give of themselves constantly in a resource capacity.[51] These parents would have a very good understanding of themselves, of others, and of the school and wider community.

The outcomes from advanced training include parent-to-parent contact, a trained pool of parents providing local leadership and more efficient and effective work at local community level. There is more time for creative work on the part of coordinators, due to the process of delegation. Most certainly there is an increased focus on the school in the community, on the forging of local links and the development of the partnership process.[52]

Local Committees
The role of local committees is defined by the Department of Education as one of advising and supporting the local coordinator.

The membership of Local Committees is divided equally between parents and representatives of voluntary and statutory agencies in the community.[53] As with the HSCL Scheme in general, so too specifically in relation to the Local Committees, the aim is to build the activity from the community upwards. It is envisaged that the work, energy, and creativity to see any project through to completion must come from parents and from community groups. It is the belief also that programmes must be practical, appropriate to the needs of the community, planned on their terms and delivered in their language. The multiplier effect was stressed from the beginning. It was, and is, the task of Local Committees to identify school related issues, at community level, and to seek to address them by working collaboratively with other interest groups. In short, the Local Committee deals with issues in the community that impinge on learning, learning in its widest sense.

Transfer needs, relating to progression from home to school and from one school level to another within the system, have been addressed by Local Committees. School attendance issues, drug awareness, anti-bullying programmes and self-image projects have also been targeted. In many instances in recent years, policy formation between parents, teachers and community personnel has been advanced through the Local Committee. The strength of the Local Committee is partnership in action. The community element was not strong initially and the observation of the National and Assistant National Coordinators from attendance at Local Committee meetings was that the professionals did the talking instead of drawing out and including the parents. In the interval between Local Committee meetings the coordinator regularly meets the 'core group'[54] of parents to facilitate the development of committee skills and to enable parents to express their point of view. In fact, all coordinators have a core group of involved parents who work with them and support the aims of HSCL. In some instances Local Committee members have done training together on the development of teams, committee work, partnership, and community development.

At present, eleven years after the inception of the HSCL Scheme, almost all schools are part of a Local Committee. A challenge to the development of their committees seems to have been a lack of clarity around the role and function of such a body, which is essentially voluntary and subject to the Board of

Management. The need for an additional committee was not obvious to many principals and coordinators since other committees often existed. However, that too is changing. The current climate and the flow of literature accepting the mutually interacting roles of community and school has opened up possibilities for the development of Local Committees.[55] In addition 'different geographical areas and groups of people dictate that there cannot be a uniform solution' when it comes to the linking of community and school.[56]

Parents and Teachers Working Together on Policy Formation

In order to strengthen links between the home and the school, coordinators work with teachers, developing deeper awareness of pupil and family circumstances, promoting the concept of parental involvement in children's learning and providing opportunities for parent-teacher interaction. Some teachers continue to explore new ways of working with parents through identifying both their expectations and concerns for children. They also involve them in class behaviour and homework codes. An emerging focus, and one that took almost three years to develop in the HSCL Scheme, was that of parents and teachers working together in policy formation.

In the spring of 1996 the principal of a large urban junior primary school facilitated the National Coordinator in working with sixteen staff members and sixteen parents. The National Coordinator in consultation with the group designed the workshops as the process evolved.[57] The local HSCL coordinator was actively involved at all stages. The following autumn the local coordinator delivered the process and outcomes as an in-career development module for coordinators. During the academic year 1996-1997 the process included two local coordinators coming to work with the experiment and continuing the process of policy formation. In March 1997 the policy outcomes in relation to 'homework' and 'good behaviour' were presented by teachers and parents at the 'regional cluster'[58] meeting. The following autumn the outcomes were presented during in-career development sessions for coordinators. At this point all coordinators were asked by the National Coordinator to work on the development of policy within their schools. The emphasis was to be on process and not on outcomes.

In the 1997-1998 school year 94 per cent of the schools in the HSCL Scheme formulated a draft policy on home, school, community relationships and practices. The emphasis was placed on the process and not on the outcome. At nine of the ten 'regional cluster' meetings in the spring of 1998 the following strengths of the policy making process were noted by principals, chairpersons, some parents and coordinators. Almost all of the points noted recurred across all the meetings in either the same or similar language. (Where a point was the exception rather than the rule this has been stated.) Participants claimed that fears about policy making between parents and teachers were 'dissolved', that parents and teachers were 'relaxed' in each other's company and that the experience was 'enjoyable' and 'very positive'. There was a sense of 'enthusiasm' and 'equality' among participants and discernible 'changes in attitude', particularly on the part of teachers.

In moving from the atmosphere to the process itself participants stated that 'the task was clear', that there was cause for 'more agreement rather than the opposite', and that there was a common 'sense of purpose' with 'similar aims' and 'aspirations'. The 'clarification of roles' made working together 'much more acceptable'. The 'commitment all round' was noted, so too was the 'exchange of ideas' while the 'listening to feelings and to fact' displayed the 'trust', 'flexibility', and 'discovering together' that typified the 'group'. One of the regional cluster groups put it succinctly: 'the process was worthwhile, simple, flexible, with whole-child development in mind'. They concluded by saying that 'the process is a model' for further work in any policy area.

There were references to the 'time' given by staff, to their 'generosity', 'honesty' and 'surprise' (at how easy it was to work together), to their being 'willing to be involved', to their 'fears being unfounded' and to the fact that teachers were 'listening to parents'. The 'report to the staff meeting' brought 'very positive comments' and there was an 'interest among the staff generally'.

The community aspect of the school was heightened in that 'primary and post-primary schools came together' for policy formation in some instances and there was 'consensus regarding the policy content' across the sectors. Teachers 'got to know other teachers' through 'inter-school' contact and this gave the staff a 'broader base'. The 'inter-school aspect also helped integration'. Cognisance was taken of 'parent-parent concerns and needs'. The 'community approach' created 'a sense of ownership' and 'stresses school values' which then became 'values owned by the community'. One of the regional cluster groups believed that they should celebrate this participation in a variety of ways.

The fact that the Board of Management 'was involved in the process', supported the coordinator', 'provided facilities' and 'took part' added an invaluable and very necessary dimension to the task.

In addition to the trust-building which took place between home, school and community, and the inter-school contacts the theme of 'affirmation', of 'self-worth and confidence building', and of having been 'energised' constantly recurred. So too did the fact of the 'parent as prime educator'. The challenges for the future of policy making included 'the finding of time', which was an issue for most regional cluster groups.

The 'involvement of fathers' and of the 'marginalised parent' will also be a challenge facing schools in the future. It was the opinion of some participants that the 'selection' of parents and teachers, which took place, in most instances, for the 1997-1998 policy sessions would need to be reviewed for the future. Parent 'expectation' has been raised regarding involvement and this needs to be 'maintained'. There was also an issue around the feasibility of bringing parents and teachers together in the 'multiple school' situation and where 'primary and post-primary schools serve the same families'. It was strongly held that staff required 'development' and that the 'workload of teachers' who were 'already stressed' should be monitored. It was pointed out that there was a need to 'implement-evaluate-update' the current draft policy document. It was stated clearly that in the policy making process, the coordinator was the key 'link agent'.

Networking

We now examine the role of the coordinator and the theory and practice of 'networking'.[59] The coordinators liaise with various voluntary and statutory bodies and groups within the community. They encourage a cohesive delivery of service in relation to parents, teachers, and community – all in the interest of the pupils. Just as the school is a significant resource to the community it serves, there are also many advantages for the school in drawing from the strengths of the community.[60] The HSCL Scheme philosophy recognises that the school on its own cannot effect meaningful change, but that it can, working collaboratively with other interest groups, ameliorate the effects of the problems associated with educational disadvantage. The links are very obvious in relation to the prevention of early school leaving.

From its inception, the scheme has emphasised the responsibility of coordinators in the area of networking and in directing parents towards existing agents and agencies already working in the community. Courses, classes and activities for parents, provided by coordinators at the behest of parents, were a source of conflict in some areas until 1995 approximately. Coordinators who have easier access to the family, through the school, were deemed to be very successful in a short space of time and this would seem a valid judgement. In other situations, it would seem that coordinators did not work diplomatically with community groups and did not adhere strictly to the principle of networking. We should not lose sight of the fact that there may have been some fear on the part of community groups of their territory being invaded. Experiences through various aspects of the scheme have highlighted the need to clarify the rights and responsibilities of various roles and thereby obviate misunderstanding and tension. It can be said that an understanding of networking, in theory and in fact, is an initial step towards the integrated delivery of service to marginalised children and their families.

The Integrated Delivery of Service to Marginalised Children and Families

As already stated in Chapter Two, both home and school are 'imperfect societies', which by implication require inclusion of the community in a serious way.[61] However, whilst calling for and recognising the need of uniting the effort of all three, it is important not to raise unrealisable expectations in the way in which we speak about integration. The Department of Education has been outspoken in advocating the integrated delivery of all programmes to marginalised children and their families. The Organisation for Economic Co-operation and Development (OECD) member countries believe that 'by working together, human services can provide more effective and appropriate services – and at a reduced cost to governments'.[62]

The Department of Education schemes, Area Development Management, The Demonstration Programme launched by the Combat Poverty Agency, The Integrated Services Process, initiated by the Department of an Taoiseach, and more recently followed by RAPID (Revitalising Areas, Planning, Investment, and Development) declare the Government's commitment to integrate services. The 'Springboard' initiative of the Department of Health and Children and programmes from Equality, Justice and Law Reform attest to the collective endeavour to develop an integrated and national response to poverty. The National Children's Strategy was the result of the collaborative work of nine Government Departments and aims 'to support a greater level of inter-agency and inter-disciplinary work as an effective way of promoting a seamless service, which is child-focused rather than service led'.[63]

Partnership 2000 clearly advocates support for the integrated delivery of service and is explicit in its message. 'The tackling of social exclusion requires an integrated approach, with full inter-sectional co-ordination, and an appropriate mid- to short-term measures ... This must be multi-dimensional and must be targeted in such a way as to reach the individuals and communities directly affected'.[64]

There is a responsibility on all Department of Education National Coordinators to ensure a high level of integration within and between schemes inspired by the Department of Education and between Department schemes and other service providers. However, it must be borne in mind that despite the best efforts at integration the outcome may be limited because of the multifaceted and complex nature of marginalisation and that of educational disadvantage within the wider frame of socio-economic disadvantage. As already stated in Chapter One, the problem for 'at risk' young people is that the factors contributing to marginalisation are so often interrelated. Hence, they reinforce each other with consuming effects on the quality of life both for the young person and the family, and indeed for the local community. When families in disadvantaged communities have just learned how to cope with one problem, the lack of progress in another area may cancel out the benefit. In addition, all activities are bound by human limitation, limitation both on the skill and personal levels of those who are most active in working to eradicate socio-economic disadvantage.

Strengths and Weaknesses of Coordinators

In the light of what we have already said about the coordinator, one could expect that a summary evaluation of the strengths and weaknesses of the coordinator would bring us close to a grasp of key strengths and weaknesses of the whole scheme. It might be helpful to get one matter out of the way, namely, the influence of the personality of the coordinator on the exercise of the role of coordinator in the scheme. The questionnaires addressed to principals, teachers, parents and Boards of Management, as well as the interviews, of the same groups, threw up only minuscule evidence of unsuitable persons having the role of coordinator.[65] In addition there was no evidence of the coordinator's personality being a block to the operation of the scheme. Further evidence that the coordinators have, up to now, been very satisfactorily selected can be found in the small number of voices which were open to – much less recommending – the suggestion that the coordinator not be a teacher.[66] Therefore, in Chapter Six, we will deal with the strengths and weakness of talented and dedicated coordinators who are not, through their personalities or approach, a cause of deficiency even though, as we shall see, there are some significant weaknesses across the board.

Evaluation Procedures

The official evaluation structures in the HSCL Scheme were operated through the Educational Research Centre 1990-1993. The ensuing report is now in two forms. Firstly, a report by the Educational Research Centre (Dublin), commissioned by the Department of Education and covering almost the first three years of the scheme.[67] Secondly, a Ph.D. thesis based on this research, in Western Michigan University two years later.[68] This research proceeds descriptively and is based on questionnaires to fifty-five primary schools in the scheme, initially for base line data. Six schools were studied in depth, with extensive interviewing and standardised achievement testing carried out in English and mathematics in first, third and fifth classes in primary schools. Thirteen post-primary schools were included in year two and three of the general evaluation.

Another Ph.D. evaluation was carried out between 1995 and 1999.[69] This evaluation differs firstly, in it being a study from within the scheme. Secondly, in that quantitative research was sought for all 182 existing schools as of 30 June, 1994. Thirdly, it differs in the focus being on the coordinator as a key innovative contribution of the Irish scheme. Fourthly, it details and evaluates in-career development. Fifthly, it carried out action research. Sixthly, it highlighted scheme shortcomings through the findings and it set out to rectify them (formative evaluation). Finally, a small comparative study with Scotland was carried out. As the 1999 evaluation was done at a later time it was appropriate to give a more extensive literature review. The two dissertations can thus be seen as complementary and the first studies in areas that will need much further research. Evaluation of the HSCL Scheme, as part of an integrated package of services of the Irish Government supported by the National Development Plan to tackle disadvantage, needs to take place.

This account can, at most, be an interim one of a scheme that is both rapidly developing in depth and rapidly expanding. Since the initiative taken by the Department of Education in 1990 was aimed at a serious need, namely children of disadvantaged families, the crucial test will not be obvious for about another five to eight years when it might be possible to conduct further research. Such research would be able to take account of completed post-primary and third level education by these children. It would also tap into employment figures, records from the Gardaí, and information available to voluntary bodies, as well as to the Departments of Social, Community and Family Affairs; Justice, Equality and Law Reform and Enterprise, Trade and Employment. After all, we should remember that the definitive evaluation of the Rutland Street Project was only made available in 1993, twenty-four years after its inception.[70] Similar findings were made with the Highscope Perry Pre-school Study later in 1993.[71]

Summary

In Chapter One we traced the strategies introduced by the Department of Education to deal with disadvantage. In Chapter Three the focus was on the HSCL Scheme. The five Aims of the scheme were listed. The philosophy of the scheme was illustrated through the framework of the twelve Basic Principles.

The hope of the Department of Education to establish partnership in education between parents, teachers and community agencies was highlighted as part of the philosophy and will be dealt with also in Chapter Four. So too was the desire of the Department of Education to promote and sustain an integrated approach to disadvantage and educational failure.

Difficulties were encountered in establishing the Basic Principles. Some of these were impatience on the part of teachers with the 'preventative' approach, a lack of in-career development for staff, an unclear view on the part of coordinators relating to 'needs analysis' and the 'networking process' and fear around the establishment of Local Committees.

Personnel and structures that provided support for the development and maintenance of HSCL were described. The advisory role of the National Steering Committee was recorded. The work of the National and Assistant National Coordinators was detailed, as was in-career development for coordinators.

Finally, the role of the local coordinator was dealt with in some depth. The Department of Education views the coordinator as a change agent. Their brief is to develop meaningful partnership processes with parents, teachers and community agencies without duplicating or replicating services. The Department of Education highlighted flexibility regarding the role of the coordinator in order to provide scope for initiative and creativity. The importance of coordinators working as a team, establishing an area profile, analysing needs, identifying and training leader parents, networking and ensuring the integrated delivery of service to marginalised children and their families was clearly established as Department of Education policy.

It can be said that the HSCL Scheme has a purposeful orientation towards partnership in education. Its activities are focused on directing the ability and talent of parents, teachers, and community towards collective endeavour. The issue of partnership, from theoretical and practical view points, will be dealt with in Chapter Four.

CHAPTER FOUR

A Crucial Insight: Partnership

AN IMPORTANT ISSUE in the contemporary world which is central to this study is partnership. As it is an emerging concept the language is not yet fixed. In particular, the notion of equality varies from author to author. Thus we can speak of the need for equality of opportunity for pupils.[1] There is also, of course, inequality that may arise from sociological and psychological opportunities leading to unequal achievement.[2] It may not always be valuable to speak about equality in the context of the contribution of the various parties to the educational enterprise. It is another matter to try to use equality around the different contributions of individuals and groups. Equality does not imply that people come from a position of equal resource or power rather 'it implies that a relationship has been formed on a basis that recognises that each has an equally important contribution to make to the whole, contributions which will vary in nature, are compatible and each of which is unique'.[3] One might find wider agreement when partnership is described in terms of a definition of roles, together with an understanding of the inherent rights and responsibilities that accompany those roles.

The salient characteristics of partnership are vision, 'goal orientation, solidarity, communication, empowerment and transformation'.[4] These elements, working in sequence or in tandem, can initiate change and growth leading to an empowerment of groups and communities. This in turn facilitates transformation, which is the central tenet of partnership.

Partnership incorporates the concept of vision. Vision can be compared to the guiding star of a scheme for the school community, the wider community or organisation.[5] Vision is essential to keep a group on target. A vision is as real as the commitment of the group is to actualising it. The greater the vision the more inevitable it is that it will never be attained. This leads to defining steps within a time frame where members are involved in the debate, exploring possibilities together, agreeing the ground rules and planning together. 'Partners may help one another in general or specific ways, but none is ever a client, because the relationship is mutual.'[6]

We now examine the concepts of partnership, power, authority and patriarchy, and empowerment. Many writers turn to M. Weber, a post Marxian theorist, sociologist, economist and political scientist when considering the areas of power and authority. For Weber, 'power' lies in the ability to get things done by enforced sanctions. 'Authority' is actually getting things done because one's orders are viewed by others as justified or legitimate. Weber claims that there are three types of authority. Traditional authority is based on the premise that the ruler has an inbuilt right to rule while charismatic authority emanates from the belief that the ruler has innate and unique gifts. Legal-rational authority is based on formal written rules and enforced by law. Weber holds that bureaucracy corresponds to the legal-rational type of authority which focuses on hierarchy, rules and rigid procedures.[7]

For T. Bentley, a theorist in the area of motivation, there are three types of power, namely, real power, role power and reflected power.[8] When acting out of real power 'employees will be using their power in ways that can materially influence organizational success'.[9] According to Block, partnership means 'to be connected to another in a way that the power between us is roughly balanced'.[10] He prefers the concept of 'stewardship', which is the 'willingness to be accountable for the well-being of the larger organization by operating in service, rather than in control'.[11] Today, the emphasis is on developing potential and using the innovative resources of all members within the organisation and indeed within the family.

Whitehead and Eaton-Whitehead from the Institute of Pastoral Studies in Chicago, believe that genuine authority expands life and makes power more abundant. They see parents as 'our first authority figures. Good parents encourage their children's first steps and support their later leaps. They learn to correct without stunting ... inviting the child into adulthood'.[12] Partnership does not do away with hierarchy because 'people at higher levels do have specialized responsibility, but it is not so much for control as it is for clarity ... of requirements ... of value-added ways of attending to a specific market'.[13]

Partnership is brought about by a consistent commitment to the demanding and painful work of human relating. Partnership invites people to share power and to welcome mutual vulnerability. It implies that there is: an ability to listen, clarity in thinking, self-understanding, a high level of motivation and commitment to conflict-resolution. Partnership also calls for the capacity to acknowledge feelings and to be compassionate. [14]

A long-term approach is required if this level of understanding and participation is to be achieved. Not only is time required to achieve participation, but genuine implementation also takes time.

Patriarchy is a belief system in which people in leadership make decisions about policy, strategy and implementation, while people in the middle and at the bottom exist to execute and implement. Often we operate this way because we are unsure of alternatives.[15] Partnership offers an option. Partnership condemns patriarchy and its practices. Block holds that the 'fundamental belief' of patriarchy is to give attention to 'maintaining control, consistency, and predictability' within organisations.[16] This process, he argues, 'may appear to be a common sense and logical approach to governance', but from another angle the demands of patriarchy for control, consistency, and predictability 'become its own obstacle'.[17]

It is important to be aware of the possible significance – conscious and unconscious – of gender differentiation.[18] One of the primary tasks of early childhood is the development of gender identity. The personal meaning of gender identity evolves long past early childhood. Gradually children make use of society's messages about being male and female and come to a sense of ownership of gender. C. Jung, famous for theories on personality, believed that women and men were designed to complement one another. He held that feminine 'traits' revolved around a woman's instinct to seek belonging and relating while the masculine ones described man's innate drive towards autonomy.[19] Contemporary psychology has brought this theory of Jung under increasing scrutiny.

Drudy and Uí Chatháin in their monograph *Gender Equality in Classroom Interaction* claim that 'Feminist research sees gender as a basic organising principle that profoundly shapes/mediates the concrete conditions of our lives'.[20] A theory 'may be defined as feminist if it can be used to challenge, counteract or change a *status quo* that disadvantages or devalues women'.[21] In *Ecclesia: A Theological Encyclopedia of the Church*, C. O'Donnell, a noted Irish and international theologian cites 'a number of factors usually found in feminist thinking as: women's experience of patriarchy; lack of equality;

discrimination'.[22] He holds that there is a division about the tactics to be employed for securing the aims of feminism and poses the question 'should I pursue human rights by insisting on the same humanity that women and men share together, or should it emphasise the difference arising from gender and thus focus on women's rights?'[23]

Within the HSCL Scheme 20 per cent of the coordinators at primary level are male with 25 per cent at post-primary level. This reflects the male/female proportion in the primary teaching profession. The parents who frequent the schools and HSCL activities are largely female. This may account for the fact that, proportionally speaking, post-primary males do not apply for the role of HSCL coordinator. In 'Where Have all the Fathers Gone?' the Bernard van Leer Foundation point to the fact that in marginalised communities women tend to hold on to the nurturing role as so much else in life has been taken from them.[24] 'Maybe they fear that men will try to dominate in the one arena in which females have firm control'.[25]

In her research on *Gender Differences in Parent Involvement in Schooling*, L. Lareau highlights the fact that 'social class provided parents with unequal resources to assist their children in schooling' and that working-class families have a 'pattern of separation between home and school'.[26] In addition, she repeatedly stated that 'the routine activities of supervising schooling overwhelmingly fell to mothers' in working-class families.[27] This was also the case in middle-class areas with fathers often citing the 'demands of their careers'.[28] Lareau points out from her research that when fathers became involved they often made 'important decisions and often took an assertive and controlling role in their interactions with female teachers' rather than a partnership approach.[29] The aim of the Bernard van Leer Foundation is to raise the status of care for children and they define it as 'a shared responsibility of all members of the community whether they work inside or outside the home'.[30]

Other angles on the relationship between partners can be noted from the works of Hirshman, Block, and Seeley. The American, A.O. Hirshman in his book *Exit, Voice and Loyalty* addresses only the issues of institutional malfunction and the human response of withdrawal. Seeley adapts the 'concepts of voice and loyalty' and changes the term 'exit' to 'choice' to accommodate both positive and negative responses.[31] If used from a partnership standpoint, Seeley's use of 'voice', which would enable parents to register disagreement with policies and practice and his use of 'choice', which would enable them to change to other institutions, would lead to empowerment of individuals and groups. For him 'loyalty' is inherent in voice and choice. 'The job of fitting voice, choice and loyalty into a sound policy for educational partnerships must be accomplished through public policy determined by citizens, legislators, school board members, community leaders and educators ... shifting the policy focus in education from bureaucratic "service delivery" to partnership'.[32]

Block holds that each person is responsible at every level for defining vision and values in the partnership situation 'Purpose gets defined through dialogue ... with each person having to make a declaration ... Each has a voice in discussing what the institution will become'.[33] For him choice is enshrined in the right to say no.

> The notion that if you stand up you will get shot undermines partnership. Partnership does not mean that you always get what you want. It means that you may lose your argument but you never lose your voice.[34]

Clearly, for these authors, the operative words are loyalty and its opposite, betrayal.

Joint accountability is another corner-stone of a partnership model. The outcomes and quality of co-operation of the institution are each person's responsibility 'the price of that freedom (partnership) is to take personal accountability for the success and failure of our unit and our community'.[35] This level of individual and corporate responsibility is outlined by V. Lombardi, the legendary football coach, when L. Iacocca, who brought Chrysler back from the brink of near bankruptcy to repayment of its controversial $1.2 billion loan, asked him about 'his formula for success'. Responding, Lombardi said 'you have to start by teaching the fundamentals' to the players. Then you ask them 'to keep in line' because the discipline of team spirit is vital. Playing as a team demands that members 'care for one another' and 'love each other'. Every time a football player goes out to play 'he's got to play from the ground up – from the soles of his feet right to his head. Every inch of him has to play'. Head and heart must play in tandem, Lombardi says and 'if you're lucky enough to find a guy with a lot of head and a lot of heart, he's never going to come off the field second'.[36]

Common interest articulated and agreed, planning together, an equal share in decision-making processes and interdependence are all part of a solidarity that is inherent in partnership and 'partnership is a central notion of solidarity'.[37] Ruane states that 'solidarity is about partnership. The partners share a common and specific vision … From this basis flows a practice which is, in essence, the pursuit of common interests. Solidarity is about involvement in common struggle'.[38] This notion of uniting in struggle is parallel to the Freirean notion of understanding the oppressed. 'Solidarity requires that one enters into the situation of those with whom one is identifying; it is a radical posture'.[39]

Partnership and Empowerment

It can be said people want to make a difference yet employers and management are often unable to take advantage of the human creativity and initiative that is available. Empowerment is a process of enabling people to acquire 'skills, knowledge and confidence' to make 'responsible choices and to carry them out in an interdependent fashion'.[40] Block would hold that the empowered person is the one who serves, the one who chooses service over self-interest and that the recipients of our service are the ones we become accountable to.[41] We can say that real power, 'empowerment', is service.

Empowerment of the local community is a strong theme running through much literature today and through all of the Bernard van Leer publications.[42] Its development is in reaction to authoritarian attitudes, or hand-outs, which can ease the distress of people, but without changing the causes of deprivation or helping people to come to full dignity or humanity. Salach, a native of Morasha, set about change and development in her own community by placing emphasis on the family and community. She enabled the local community to identify its needs and arrive at a solution through self-help. in this way she developed local leadership.[43]

The main thrust of the Bernard van Leer Foundation (BvLF) is its focus on the child. This enables their educational theorists to make important contributions to the interrelation of the professional teacher and the parent. Thus in the study the *Parent as Prime Educator*, we note that the role of the professional is not to teach the parents but to 'widen their common meeting ground' and in particular to develop a teaching-learning situation so as 'to enable the validation of the parents' knowledge and self-confidence'.[44] Paz refers to these parents as para-professionals. She concludes that their involvement transfers them from being passive and dependent to becoming active community members.[45] Salach expresses the same view-point about empowerment of local people when she says that 'due to their ability to create direct ties with parents and children in the community, they personified the process of replacing apathy and dependency with a responsible and active approach ... these women were also the harbingers of future change in the community'.[46]

Empowerment, according to Freire, releases a new power in the individual to act upon and to transform the world. This power comes through 'a new awareness of self, has a new sense of dignity, and is stirred by a new hope.'[47] Freire's theory of working 'with' and not 'for' finds further expression in a transformation of life that can be realised when 'those hands – whether of individuals or entire peoples – need to be extended less and less in supplication ... they become hands which work and, by working transform the world'.[48] Freire points out that when the oppressors cease to interfere even in the name of 'false generosity' and allow the oppressed to achieve transformation, oppressors and oppressed become part of 'the process of permanent liberation'.[49] F. Pignatelli, when Director of Education in the then Strathclyde area of Scotland, put it succinctly at a conference in Dublin in 1992 where he claimed that 'partnership can be defined as identifying, releasing and sharing our own gifts and the gifts of others, not only gifts of personality but gifts of experience as well'.[50]

Whether partnership is a desired and feasible end-state, an attainable aspiration or whether it turns out to be unrealistic, a responsibility still lies on all educators 'to become more responsive to the needs, wishes and experience of parents and children ... the development of an honest partnership that recognizes important differences as well as shared concerns'.[51] As we have noted, the call of partnership is for personal transformation that would hopefully lead to the recognition of strengths and concerns of individuals and to genuine interdependence. Structural transformation will be demanded in order to bring roles and plans into greater congruence with values. This will demand, in the words of Block, 'a choice for service, with partnership and empowerment as basic governance strategies'.[52]

The Irish Experience

Partnership in Practice: Interviews

During the interviews, principals, core groups of parents and the coordinators themselves were asked their opinions on the coordinators and on their role as a link agent within the HSCL Scheme.[53] Chairpersons and a further group of randomly selected parents, all in the sixteen selected schools, were asked about the same issues through the form of a short questionnaire.

The interviews sought insights and information about how self-aware the coordinators were regarding their strengths, their challenges, their ability to communicate, their ability to build relationships, and hence their ability to interrelate. Evidence of how this self-awareness can lead to a deeper awareness of others and in turn to an appreciation of difference was also sought. This appreciation of difference emerges if the coordinator has the ability to see and hear others as different individuals, and it is indicated through the 'values and beliefs that the coordinator seems to hold and how he/she sees the scheme'. The ability of the coordinator to communicate, and thus make contact, was a central issue for exploration during interviews. Contact can promote good relationships, enthusiasm, proactive ideas, and can lead to the multiplier effect and thence to a delegation process. Quality contact also leads to the development of trust. However, trust alone will neither develop interrelatedness nor partnership. If sufficient time and effort have been afforded to the development of the self, leading to greater awareness of others and to appreciation of difference, then trust can grow. As outlined earlier, partnership can begin to develop when home and school, parents and teachers value their association with each other in the name of the pupil. 'The presence of respect turns a group of associates into a team', which can be as small as the parent-teacher-pupil team.[54] The quality of mutual acceptance found in the principal-coordinator team, the teacher-coordinator team, the parent-coordinator team and the principal-teacher-parent-pupil-coordinator team can enhance the enjoyment of mutual roles and can lead to greater benefits for the pupil.

In relation to the interviews with parents, it can be said that the feelings of the parents are sometimes as important as the information they convey. The vivid colloquial style of some of the answers has been retained to catch something of the flavour of the interview.

The Coordinator as a Person

Principals interviewed spoke in very positive personal terms about the coordinator. Comments made by principals incorporated the following. The coordinator was 'ideal for the role', was 'warm and thoughtful', had a 'sense of vision', was 'very committed and enthusiastic', was 'compassionate', was 'full of ideas' and was 'a good listener'. It was further said that the coordinator had 'built up a lot of support for the school' had 'done fantastic work' but that the 'workload was too heavy'. Another principal stated that 'the coordinator was the non-threatening, friendly face of the school'.

Core groups of parents who were interviewed made comments of a personal nature. Included were that the coordinator was 'super-confident', had the 'gift of the gab', was 'friendly and relaxed', was 'approachable, very caring, enthusiastic, and good fun'. Other parents spoke of the fact that the coordinator was 'brilliant, one of ourselves, down to earth and very understanding'. A core group spoke of the coordinator being 'so gentle', while in another situation the parents spoke of the coordinator being 'very, very assertive and very diligent'. At another interview the parents said that the coordinator was 'bubbly, had a great personality, and tries to do anything'. A final comment in this area was that the coordinator was 'very welcoming the minute you saw him'.

Many coordinators interviewed made personal comments. They spoke of themselves as being 'warm, approachable, and not very teachery'. Another coordinator said that she came across as 'friendly, approachable, hard-working sincere and supportive'. Others saw themselves as 'modelling hope', as 'non-judgemental', as 'competent', as having 'no problem' at their work or in their relationships and many mentioned the fact that they were 'a good listener'.

The above comments of principals, core groups of parents and of coordinators were common among the responses.

The Coordinator as Link Agent

The link role of the coordinator is central to their work. Principals acknowledged that they either had a 'very good working relationship' with the coordinator, or that the coordinator was 'seen by staff and principal as infinite support', or that the coordinator was 'very, very helpful in a crisis' or that they were 'personally very pleased'. One principal believed that the coordinator made the 'principal's life easier'. Some principals stated that there was 'some fear initially' on the part of teachers but that now they were 'open, receptive and warm' but that 'work [needed] to be done on teachers taking ownership'. Finally a principal claimed that the 'coordinators came across as very useful' and that 'the teacher finds them valuable in relation to absenteeism'. A principal said that the coordinator saw 'parents as an extension of children's education', while another principal claimed, in a positive way, that the coordinator was 'very defensive of her parents' and that 'the parents' point of view must be got across at all costs'.

From the foregoing it can be said that principals valued the coordinator as 'ideal for the role' and as possessing many personal qualities such as warmth, commitment, and enthusiasm. It emerged that principals were enjoying a 'very good working relationship' with the coordinator. It could be interpreted that a particular type of person applied for the role of coordinator or that principals made a wise choice when appointing the coordinator, and/or that training and motivation of coordinators went hand in hand. Principals seem to rely on coordinators as important people in the life of the school. One might question statements from the principal in relation to the coordinator who 'makes life easier for the principal' or who is 'very, very helpful in a crisis' or who is 'invaluable in relation to absenteeism'. Taking the proactive and preventative nature of the HSCL Scheme into consideration, these statements reveal the immediate needs of principals.

Core Groups of parents spoke about their awareness of the coordinator through his/her work. Issues that arose were that the coordinator was 'one of the group', was 'a friend', got 'involved with parents', 'does the courses with you' and was 'not a snooty one, or high and mighty'. Another core group said that 'it takes a very special person to be a home, school, liaison person'. Parents noted also that coordinators 'try to bring the quieter parents in' and that they were 'very encouraging'. Core groups of parents valued the coordinator's personal and work traits. For parents, the coordinator was approachable, diligent, very understanding and non-authoritarian. It would appear from this that the coordinator was very accepted by parents in the core group, at least.

One coordinator said that staff would view her as 'organised and talented', another believed that the staff would see her as unafraid in trying 'to build on strengths and opportunities available to staff'. Three other coordinators gave opinions in this area and they were that they would still be viewed 'as some sort of ambulance service'. However, the staff would approach them 'much more than in the beginning', and there was appreciation of the fact that coordinators 'try to answer their needs'. The phrases that came up for coordinators regarding their relationship with parents were: 'very well known', 'supportive to parents, very comfortable with parents', parents were 'comfortable talking to me' and 'I [the coordinator] don't listen enough'. Coordinators held positive views about themselves as persons and in relation to their work. They viewed themselves as 'warm', 'non-judgemental' and 'competent'. They were also realistic in that they were aware of the need 'to listen more' and to bring staff on board.

Values and Beliefs of the Coordinator

We now examine the values and beliefs of the coordinator as perceived by principals, by the coordinators themselves and by chairpersons.

Ten of the sixteen principals named appreciating parents in the 'child's education' or 'parents as an integral part of the whole education process' or simply 'valuing the parent', as part of the values and belief system of the coordinator. Other values held by the coordinator, according to principals, were those of 'great compassion', a 'deep Christian philosophy', a 'deep understanding of the ethos of the school', and a 'belief in the long term strategy and a holding out of hope for the future'. Qualities of coordinators named by principals were 'commitment', 'loyalty', 'infinite support', and the seeing of 'good in everybody'. One principal held that the coordinator's view 'complied' with his own 'that the school should be a very real support to community', while another claimed that as principal he had 'to be careful where they [the coordinators] are leading'.

The rationale underpinning the value system of one coordinator was that she would 'help parents to help themselves and to help children', while another coordinator stated 'I believe completely in it [the HSCL Scheme] as a preventative model'. 'Respect' was a value for coordinators, 'the most profound thing is respect' and 'you have to be seen to give respect'. This was echoed by another coordinator 'I would like to see all children treated with respect ... parents treated with respect by teachers. I would like to close the gap between teachers and parents'. The foregoing impressions were reflected throughout the interviews with coordinators.

One coordinator had, for many years, visited the homes of his pupils and had given the use of his home phone number to parents and pupils for two hours each evening, as a class teacher. He had spent years as a coordinator at the time of interview. He said that keeping 'in touch with the home and with parents' was 'the most powerful aid you could have to a successful life as a teacher'. This coordinator was convinced of the value of linking home, community, and school, of building up 'a community in the school and the school as a service to community'. He concluded by saying 'I have read about the value of home, school and community in books, but I lived through it first hand and that makes the difference'.

Another coordinator's 'values/beliefs' were to have parents 'more involved in education in its broadest sense ... as a lifelong process...not just academic work ... learning to be relaxed ... [to] make life better for everyone'. For other coordinators the big issue was 'the empowerment of parents and the opening of teachers' eyes, very slowly'. This, one concluded, must be done in a non-patronising way.

The focus on the 'disadvantaged child' was in evidence during the interviews. An interviewee claimed that her motivators included the holding out of 'help to the disadvantaged children' as 'they don't get a fair deal out of the education system', while children like her own, 'get so much'. It was also held by coordinators that parent experiences of school 'had to be worked on' because these bad experiences are 'bound to rub off on their children'. The chairpersons of the sixteen schools selected for an in-depth study were circulated regarding the 'values and beliefs' of the coordinator. The responses from chairpersons have been drawn together as follows:

- 40.9 per cent said that 'empowerment of parents' was a value for the coordinator
- 38.6 per cent held that 'partnership' was a value
- 09.1 per cent spoke of 'community development'
- 06.8 per cent maintained that 'staff - school' change was a value
- 04.5 per cent claimed that 'benefits for children' was a 'value/belief' of the coordinator.[55]

[Percentages rounded up/down to 0.1 per cent]

How the Coordinator Sees the HSCL Scheme

In this section we shall outline what principals and parent core groups perceive as the view of the coordinator about the HSCL Scheme. The coordinator's views are also noted.

Principals gave very positive responses in relation to the views of coordinators on the HSCL Scheme. Ten of the sixteen principals spoke of the coordinator as building 'a relationship-bridge-link' between home, school, and community 'through parents for children'. Individual comments from principals were that their own coordinator saw the work as 'extraordinarily worth while' and that he/she worked hard giving 'attention to detail and everyday commitment'. The coordinator saw the scheme as 'very valuable and very necessary', saw the scheme as 'an ongoing thing to combat poverty and disadvantage', had made 'a solid start' and because of that the principal could say, 'I believe in it myself'.

One principal held that the coordinator saw her role as 'her vocation in life', was 'totally converted and committed to the scheme', was 'never off duty and was very accommodating'. For another principal the coordinator was 'not a bit selfish', 'believed wholeheartedly' in the scheme, had a 'great understanding of people' and worked on 'developing a camaraderie even with local people'.

Personal comments from principals included that the coordinator was 'a fine quality person' and worked with 'a very genuine, sincere, open desire'. One principal said that she could not fulfil the role of coordinator herself, 'I couldn't do what she's doing'. Another principal said that he 'couldn't run the school at present without the coordinator'.

Comments from core groups of parents spanned job enjoyment for the coordinator, job qualities of the coordinator and the clear job focus of the coordinator. Four core groups spoke of the job enjoyment of the coordinators, 'she loves it ... she likes working with parents ... she's very friendly ... like a friend but she's very professional'. Another core group claimed 'she's getting enjoyment out of what is happening ... you'd have to enjoy it to do it right'. The third core group held that 'they enjoy their work ... enjoy being with parents ... an awful lot of hard work in it ... even working after school hours'. One can gather the sense of self worth of the parents who believe that the coordinators enjoy working with them and they acknowledge the energy and commitment given by the coordinators.

Job qualities of coordinators, listed by parents on five occasions, included he is 'patient, a low key person, [has] great understanding ... the boys always liked him...he's very approachable, listens to everything' and 'is always available'. Another core group held that 'communication on a personal level is very high', and the coordinator 'will get back to you day or night'. Other parents spoke of the fact that the coordinator had built up 'a personal relationship with kids and parents' and concluded with 'he had a very good personality' and 'he never resorted to corporal punishment'. The fact that the coordinator 'gets frustrated' was named by one core group while at the same time 'she does push things' and was 'dedicated' were also acknowledged.

The clear focus of the coordinator was intimated by eight different core groups and in turn this showed how the coordinator had communicated to parents the vision of the scheme. While one core group held that the coordinator 'could do with an assistant', they concluded by saying 'we are all assistants, she is facilitating us, helping to close the gap that exists in the communication between home and school'. This portrays a very focused outlook on the part of parents who would be categorised as marginalised. We note the opening up of the communication process and that of delegation 'we are all assistants'. Another group spoke of how the coordinator helped to clarify with parents and teachers their respective roles resulting in 'we are all kind of like friends now, all for the children'. Parents were clear that 'the number one aim, is the children'.

A further emphasis on the role focus was detected through a coordinator going 'out of her way to accommodate people', helping parents to become 'involved in the school' and 'building community'. This involvement, parents believed, had repercussions for the pupils 'who are more secure' who are 'going to the library as a result' and whose parents read to children 'every day'. The following quote sums up this report from core groups and also outlines how focused the coordinator is and has enabled the parents to become: 'Her whole life tells us that we are partners in the education of children. There was no link. The school is more open because of her'.

In relation to how coordinators saw the scheme the following can be stated. All coordinators had very positive comments about the HSCL Scheme and all admit that their perception of parents, teachers, possibilities and personal power had changed. Individual coordinators said that they were happy about the scheme', had 'learned patience', that it was a 'great [scheme] locally and nationally' and that it was 'exceptionally well run'. Coordinators held that they were 'trying to reach those parents they haven't reached already, thinking about teachers too, that they haven't got on board'. It appeared that coordinators were more content with the 'long term' aim of the scheme' and were aware of the 'huge change in schools although there was 'still a long way to go'. Coordinators were 'increasingly sympathetic to principals, and less sympathetic to teachers, sometimes embarrassed to be a teacher'. This statement sprang from the positive experience that a coordinator had while working with parents. She ended by saying 'you'd nearly want to do it [liaison work] first, before you go for teaching'.

Some coordinators could not 'imagine ... how we could function without HSCL'. It had become 'an integral part of the school and of community life ... it means so much to so many people ... it is the spearhead for developments'. This coordinator recommended that 'we continue' with HSCL activities 'quietly in the background'. Coordinators were aware that parents now 'see the school as non-threatening, as a community resource', and that 'their views are now valued'. It was also held that 'staff were beginning to feel more at ease with parents'. Another coordinator said that two staff members had moved to the point of having 'parents in the classroom'. It was the conviction of some coordinators that one cannot talk 'about partnership in education unless parents are invited in and a space [provided] for them in policy making' procedures.

Coordinators have raised key issues in development showing that they are focused in their role. Foremost among their aims are trying to reach the marginalised and being content with the long-term aim of the HSCL Scheme. Being aware of scheme structures, locally and nationally, and owning the fact that liaison had become an integral part of school and community life are key aspects of liaison. Having the insight to carry out liaison duties quietly in the background, while acknowledging the difficulty of including staff in HSCL Scheme practices are invaluable skills.

Coordinators acknowledged that their perceptions had changed and developed since the HSCL Scheme started. Individuals said: 'I feel grounded in myself', 'I see where parents are coming from now', 'I see it [the HSCL Scheme] as something continually evolving' and 'it is actually happening, before this the vision was not there and we were striving after it'. Coordinators found that 'the emergence of parents as ring leaders and the support they can give to other parents' was enlightening. One coordinator thought it was going to be easier to change things', but there was 'no easy recipe' he added. That there was more 'openness' among teachers now 'because they see that the parent can help' was commented on by some coordinators. The movement from 'great numbers' of parents attempting courses to the development of 'partnership', and the 'empowerment of parents as first educators' was a quality change according to coordinators. A final comment from a coordinator can act as summary. She expressed the wish 'that everyone, myself and teachers, would be convinced of the power within and the ability to do'.

Communication on the Part of the Coordinator

The ability of the coordinator to communicate and thus make contact was a central issue during the interviews. As already stated, contact can promote good relationships, enthusiasm, a proactive work method leading to use of the delegation process, which in turn activates trust. When mutual respect is present there is hope of developing a partnership way of working. We shall examine, firstly, the response of principals, core groups of parents and of the coordinators themselves in relation to the coordinator's leadership.

Within the HSCL Scheme the word 'react' has almost a technical meaning from received usage. It is the opposite to being proactive and it does not mean an instinctive reaction, which is a common meaning in colloquial speech. While carrying out HSCL duties a proactive approach on the part of the coordinator is deemed vital in the philosophy of this 'preventative scheme'. In contrast, many schools in the past have been reactive to situations and people. Though they are not necessarily always exclusive the interviews sought to determine whether the coordinator was primarily proactive as leader, rather than reactive. In addition the research focused largely on the leadership of the coordinator, of the coordinator as a link agent. Hence the need to question interviewees about the coordinator's communication ability.

Eleven of the sixteen principals interviewed were clear that the coordinator was 'leading' within the school and community while five principals saw the coordinator as 'leading' and 'reacting'. One principal defined 'leading' as the coordinator being 'expert and seen to be expert by teachers, parents and myself'. Another principal identified the coordinator as 'very much a leader', holding a 'long term view', creating an 'ease' around the school with 'no pressure for parents, school or children' and as being 'very concerned about staff ... parents and school needs'. A further insight was along the same lines, with the addition that 'teachers were beginning to work a lot more with parents, and as a result children were benefiting'. A principal held that an experienced coordinator had 'almost a responsibility for leadership'. A different type of emphasis came from a principal who held that since the role of the coordinator was a new one, the coordinator was 'a very valuable witness for other teachers'. Furthermore, 'by taking on the role, by being faithful to the role, by staying with it and with the vision of the HSCL Scheme', coordinators expressed leadership qualities.

Sixteen out of the eighteen coordinators expressed the view that they saw themselves as 'leading' rather than 'reacting'. Two coordinators said that whilst initially they generally 'reacted', they led in 'minor things'. Some comments from coordinators give us a flavour of their leadership role. One coordinator held that in so far as parents are availing of courses 'I see myself as leader ... a quiet type of leader, quietly influencing individual members of staff'. Another coordinator commented 'I would be challenging and questioning parents and teachers about themselves or their role or what they are doing, and trying to show a way forward, leading people towards their own answer'. For still another coordinator the comment was that 'probably I would lead, a natural instinct to move to the front of the group and take responsibility'. Coordinators held that they are 'constantly opening up new initiatives', that they see 'planning as very important' and that they see themselves 'primarily as a leader'. A final comment from a coordinator was that 'hopefully leading, and learning where to lead by reacting'.

The above comments illustrate many aspects of the leadership role within schools: leading parents to their own learning and to their own answers, quietly being an influence to teachers, challenging both parents and teachers, taking on personal responsibility as coordinator, opening up new initiatives, and being involved in planning. While the leadership instinct was strong, and was proactive, many coordinators added that 'sometimes you need to react'. 'I'm sure there are times when I react' (instead of being proactive), 'but I react … if I'm asked to take something on board'. The spirit in which the coordinators seem to react to situations would not be at odds with the vision of the HSCL Scheme.

While core groups were asked many questions about the coordinator's leadership and communication they were not asked the one on 'leading' and 'reacting'. However, through the 'feelings about the HSCL Scheme' named by core groups the leadership/facilitation role of the coordinator can be deduced. Core groups claimed that there was 'a lot more communication, a lot more ease of access, a lot more help, someone to go to'. Parents held that 'for a long time parents were afraid to go to school, we only went for trouble or for parent-teacher meetings. We didn't look forward to it'. For parents, 'breaking down the barriers in the school is the big thing', while another group said that 'she tells us the teachers' perspective and helps us to work along with them'. Parents felt that 'it makes a difference to children that they know you are there'. As a parent 'if you had a problem you'd discuss it with the coordinator and see what she had to say and maybe she would help organise with the teacher for you'. A similar point from another core group: 'if you are not comfortable going to a principal or teacher, you have the HSCL coordinator to go to, and parents feel more comfortable with her if they have a problem or anything like that'.

Parents thought that the 'aims of the teachers are clearer, you are hearing the two sides instead of feeling it's you against the teacher'. The coordinator was viewed as 'a lifeline for parents' while attending classes 'gives you confidence in the school'. The coordinator and his/her work in the HSCL Scheme enables parents 'to give more time' to children, 'helps the children get over the problems and remain in school', 'children like to feel parents are doing classes', and 'children love seeing you in school'. These points were made by almost all core groups. The courses for parents promoted by coordinators were viewed as 'brilliant', 'absolutely fantastic', and 'very valuable and relevant'. One parent who found the coordinator 'fantastic' and held that he should be put 'on a pedestal' saw courses for parents as 'a load of bull'. This was an isolated observation. The leadership role of the coordinator seems evident through the above quotes. This section on the coordinator can be summed up by a core group which spanned a primary and post-primary school. This group claimed to be 'very privileged' to have coordinators 'because without the scheme we wouldn't be here today'.

Perceptions of Principals Regarding the Coordinator's Communication

Fifteen of the sixteen principals interviewed had very positive comments regarding the communication of the coordinator with principal and parents. Some had reservations, as we shall see, in relation to communication with staff. One principal held the view that 'the whole thing has been sold to the staff here'. This principal claimed that since the 'school is owned by the local community, staff would feel somewhat reassured that because of the scheme the parents understanding of school would be accurate'. However, the views of parents in this school were not as hopeful, as we shall see later.

The views of fifteen principals will shed light on how the coordinator's communication is perceived and on how he/she has managed to communicate the inspiration and practicalities of the scheme. The comments from principals were as follows: One principal held that communication with him was 'A1', and that the scheme was 'adequately announced among the parent body'. He held that the teachers were 'neutral rather than positive', that there would be difficulty with the scheme being accepted 'as an integral part' of school life because it was 'not aimed at children', yet, 'ironically [there was] a lot less confrontation between teachers and parents'. In describing the coordinators' communication, many principals used phrases such as 'very good', 'much better than me', 'very good and very tactful', 'a good communicator ... very clearly focused', 'a bridge person', 'good, with some excellent', 'generally good', and 'very good rapport'.

Principals held that work still needed to be done with staff, as there was a 'problem about the way teachers perceive things ... teachers feel that the coordinator is possibly not taking their problem seriously'. From another principal the view was that it is 'slower telling teachers', while for someone else the view was that 'earlier on, the teachers weren't open'. Again we note a principal who said that the 'messenger is giving the message but they [the staff] are not hearing'. This principal held that it 'suits teachers better' to have the coordinator working on absenteeism issues. Still another example was from a principal who gave an 'overall yes' to the coordinator in communicating the inspiration and practicalities of the scheme, but admitted that there was still 'some distance to go' and that 'parents' would be more aware than the wider 'school community'.

We shall now examine the views of the fifteen core groups in relation to how well the coordinator has communicated the aim of the HSCL Scheme to parents. Statements from parents span the coordinator's communication in general, including that done during home visitation. Some groups claimed that parents were 'very aware of the scheme' and that people who 'have an opinion' were 'listened to'. Communication of information was good in that 'letters are sent home' and there is information 'in church newsletters'. The 'coordinator stood out [at the school door] every morning and showed us where to go' and aimed at 'getting parents involved' and it was 'not unusual to see coordinators on the road'. The coordinator also 'visited homes', 'phones you' and 'everyone is met at the very same level'. The coordinator was 'constantly training parents to help each other and other parents...when facilitating we're not solving people's problems or telling groups' how to do things.

On the other hand a small number of core groups held that it would 'take years for the school to be looked at as a safe place ... our generation were intimidated by the education authorities'. Core groups claimed that the coordinator had 'a very hard job' because 'people who are underprivileged find it hard to mix' and 'their own experience of school may be a bad experience'. The core groups were also realistic in that there are 'always some you won't reach' and the lack of interest on the part of parents around their own involvement was obvious while at the same time 'they want the child to do well'.

Fifteen out of the eighteen coordinators interviewed perceived their communication with parents to be 'good' or 'very good' and as the giving of 'quality listening time'. A few coordinators held that their communication was 'honest sincere and down to earth', while another coordinator hoped that people would come to him 'anytime within limits'. Since another coordinator had 'explained' her 'position very carefully' to parents she was not asked 'to compromise' her 'professional status'. Coordinators believed that 'teachers were less accessible', and that 'at the start [there was] an area of suspicion about what was going on'. One coordinator held the view of being 'a quiet communicator with teachers', while another claimed that the 'barrier is breaking down'. A 'concern' for one coordinator was the fact that 'teachers would expect to hear more from home visitation' than the coordinator was free to share. One coordinator held that if 'the outcome' of her communication did not meet her expectations, if parents did not 'turn up to courses', then the communication was not 'clear'. This thinking would seem flawed as there could be very many reasons why people might not attend.

In relation to the communication of the inspiration and practicalities of the HSCL Scheme some coordinators held that it is difficult to inform staff. Coordinators believed that staff may 'know the rationale [of HSCL], but they might not necessarily accept it'. Coordinators held that in some staff rooms 'there is a trouble shooting mentality' and the coordinator is asked to be involved in crisis work. It was the belief of coordinators that in the case of some teachers 'there is resistance ... they don't want to hear and reluctantly they are watching and waiting to see how it's developing [HSCL work] ... if it progresses then they move a little closer'. According to coordinators, staff members are 'not really interested ... not inclined to move out further to parents...they leave me to do my thing'.

Readiness for change on the part of teachers featured for coordinators who said that the 'main body of people here heard the message, and they respond at various stages in their own way'. For other coordinators the view was that staff 'feel well informed' about the HSCL Scheme and that teachers 'are very supportive now and in agreement now with the whole thrust and aims of the scheme'. One coordinator held that the principal was 'neutral-sceptical' and had become 'supportive-pro' HSCL.

Regarding the communication of the aims and thrust of the HSCL Scheme to parents some of the comments of coordinators are as follows: 'anything I do, unless it is to maximise parental involvement, it's not worth doing', and 'parents have got as far as seeing more value in education'. 'Success' for one coordinator was 'in the number of people who contact me … if success is measured by voting with your feet … they come to me'.

The sixteen chairpersons were asked if the coordinator 'had managed to communicate adequately the inspiration and practicalities of the scheme' to the Board of Management, to parents, to teachers, to others in the community, and to the chairperson. In the following Table we note the responses from chairpersons:

Table 4.1 Has the Coordinator Communicated Adequately the Inspiration and Practicalities of the HSCL Scheme? Chairpersons' Response

	Yes	No	Unsure
Board of Management	87.5	12.5	0.0
Parents	93.8	0.0	6.3
Teachers	100.0	0.0	0.0
Community personnel	50.0	43.8	6.3
Chairperson	87.5	12.5	0.0

[Percentages rounded up by 0.1 per cent in two instances]

The view of chairpersons that coordinators had communicated adequately the vision and practicalities of the HSCL to all teachers does not seem justified in the light of other evidence.[56] A high percentage of chairpersons spoke in the affirmative regarding the coordinators' communication. However, their view that 100 per cent of teachers were adequately informed regarding the HSCL Scheme would not appear accurate from the experience of the author or from the interview data which revealed that a stunning 54 per cent of teachers had no understanding of partnership.[57]

The Type, Frequency and Clarity of Communication

Among the principals, thirteen stated that they preferred verbal communication with the coordinator, while three used the written form. Fifteen coordinators favoured verbal communication with the principal, with six favouring written communication. There were three coordinators who used both methods. Twelve principals communicated through informal means, while eight used formal methods. There were five principals who used the two ways to communicate. All coordinators, excluding one, used informal methods of communication, five used formal methods, with four coordinators using both forms of communication. In summary the preference of principals and coordinators for communicating with each other was verbal and informal. This is in keeping with the lack of value placed on formal evaluation structures.[58]

In the following section we note the responses from principals relating to 'adequate information in a clear way and on a regular basis' from the coordinator. Twelve principals stated that they 'definitely' had a 'timetable, planning and records' from the coordinator. Other phrases used were 'no matter where she is, she is working', and 'I love the days she's here'. A further principal stated the need for 'a little more' information, 'a general outline' from the coordinator. The two remaining principals claimed that if they lacked information it was their 'own fault' and one held 'I don't always listen' to the coordinator.

Twelve of the fifteen core groups of parents were very positive about the frequency and the clarity of information they received. The following statements give us a flavour of the views of core groups. Parents said that the 'note system allows for open discussion', and that 'children bring letters ... you can come to school for more information'. 'We get constant

information on everything' parents said, 'ah yes, from courses
to head lice, all notified straight away'.

While another core group claimed that 'there's definitely a
better attitude there now', they also held that 'ordinary parents
need more communication'. This group, who had been
responsible for publishing the school newsletter until transition
year pupils took it over, 'wanted more information'. Still
another core group said 'in general we don't get anything
[information] from the principal, the coordinator gives it all to
us'. They had been involved in fundraising for the school and
claimed that 'where it [money] goes we don't know' and 'we
need to know the total'. The final core group held that
'communication is good [in the schools] by the coordinators'
but that 'if you have a problem with a teacher you have to
complain to another teacher'. Parents held that this practice is
'futile' and that 'an independent person' is required.

On the whole, coordinators had made efforts to
communicate with all parties, although most would say 'that
the outcome from teachers left a lot to be desired'. A small
number admitted 'deficiencies', the need 'to improve' or 'to
work on' communication procedures. Coordinators said that
principals were 'very well informed', that 'parents know as
much as they need to know' and that 'an end of year report
[was given] to each staff member'. One coordinator held that 'I
try to give plenty of information' and that 'parent core groups
have plenty of information'. Another coordinator said that
whilst non-core group members had information about
courses, classes, and home visitation, there was still a gap with
teachers. One coordinator put it succinctly in claiming that
'parents have the clearest view, principals have a good overall
view and teachers are least familiar with my work'. While
'accurate information on everything' was given to the base
principal, the second principal 'isn't always available or doesn't

want my timetable' a coordinator claimed. Time was spent
with teachers sharing information 'hoping to inspire them and
give them support'.

Difficulties in the Area of Communication

The interviews sought information regarding difficulties in
communication from principals, core groups and from
coordinators themselves.

Eight of the fifteen principals recounted no difficulty in their
communication with the coordinator, 'I have no unvoiced
feeling ... we have established an easy relationship' and 'she is a
good communicator'. Principals held that 'as a staff we're very
communicative and happy together'. Other principals said that
'communication was very difficult' in a large staff, that
'generally things are OK ... sometimes you'd be told, sometimes
you have to ask', and voiced the need to have matters
'documented'. The usual statement that 'the parents we want
sometimes don't come in' was voiced. While another principal
said that 'only the touchy people' claimed that communication
was not good. There were 'difficulties a lot of the time' because
'the teacher focus is the class' and the 'coordinator is so focused
in a wider direction'. In one case, the coordinator and principal
were 'strong minded people'. However, the principal claimed
that the coordinator 'does defer' to the 'wishes' of the principal
who 'from time to time had to mould/direct [the coordinator]
in a kind of dictatorial way'.

Almost all core groups of parents recorded difficulties in
communicating with the school while all were highly
complimentary of the coordinator. Views of core groups can
be summarised as follows: 'if I had a problem I wouldn't
hesitate going to the coordinator', 'there is no person like the
home-school coordinator' and 'school would not run without
the coordinator'. Another comment from a core group was

that: 'you can say anything to her ... the coordinator is the only link you have really [because] teachers haven't got time'.

Difficulties recounted by core groups were that some parents were very shy and that it was difficult to bridge the gap when a new lot of children begin in September. Core groups claimed that 'a lot of parents would feel left out' while for others it was 'difficult to get our suggestions done, [we were] listened to, but things were difficult to achieve'. Core groups held that 'parents don't get enough recognition from public bodies and from the community'.

Coordinators claimed that the 'only problem was lack of time', that 'there was a difficulty in reaching parents ... and teachers' and that the 'agencies were very annoying' regarding form-filling – 'it's not what they do, but the way that they do it'. Coordinators claimed that because they know 'parents now on a personal level', there is 'no problem' even if 'the message is sticky' and that the 'biggest difficulty I would find is with staff', who are 'unfortunately under great pressures'. 'Parents would be the most positive' about the HSCL Scheme. 'To an extent some teachers lack understanding of the scheme and some have got little or no in-career development' and 'it takes time to be accepted within staff and trusted'. It was held by some coordinators that 'important decisions were made without consultation' on the part of the principal while the staff communicated well with the coordinator.

The Development by the Coordinator of a Sense of Team, Interrelatedness and Partnership

While we have been trying to establish, throughout the interviews, whether the sense of team was present or not, we will focus directly on it in this section.

Feelings about the Most Important Issues for the Coordinator

We shall examine what principals and core groups felt were 'the most important issues for the coordinator' and what coordinators felt the important issues were for themselves. With the 'issues' as backdrop we shall then proceed to look at the 'ways' in which the coordinator fostered partnership.

Principals felt that the 'important issues' for coordinators were: 'to be seen in a positive light by parents', to develop 'parent confidence and self esteem' through 'classes', to have the HSCL Scheme viewed 'as an integral part of the school' and 'to believe strongly in the value of what [they were] doing' as coordinators. Principals also felt that coordinators wanted to be involved 'in the area of most need', 'to place the school in the community', to meet the 'marginalised' through home visitation, to initiate the process of 'organising', 'coordinating', 'networking' and 'training' and 'to have more male involvement' among parents. One principal sums the foregoing up by saying that the coordinator's role is one of 'empowering parents ... she is the one they would go to', there is 'no red tape attached' to the coordinator. Another principal's view is that the coordinator 'doesn't feel the full impact [of the work], I get reactions from teachers, pupils and parents'. A further viewpoint was the hope a principal had that someone would take time to say 'well done' to the coordinator.

Core groups felt that 'important issues' for the coordinator were: 'getting to know people and being there for people', providing 'courses' and a 'parents' room' and going on 'home visitation, a quiet but very important part' of the work. Other important issues according to the core groups were 'bringing parents together ... [hearing] views about the school, the system and everything ... reaching out for parents who need a break', 'explaining what's happening in the Department of

Education ... Acts, and Relationships and Sexuality Education (RSE) ... your rights as parents' and communicating 'between home and school ... somebody that sees the overall picture'.

Instead of naming 'important issues' for the coordinator, some core groups listed the qualities of the coordinator. Some of the qualities named were that the coordinator was 'available', 'listens', 'has confidence', was 'friendly', was 'a great organiser', 'gets back to you', was 'very confidential', was a 'good explainer', was 'reliable' was 'responsible' was 'a person you can approach' and 'trust' someone who 'never puts anyone down'.

Some of the 'most important issues' voiced by coordinators were getting 'parent participation in children's education', having them 'consistent in attending' and to ensuring 'the involvement of parents in the school in a number of ways'. Coordinators also claimed to involve 'everybody, but most of all the teachers'. Another important issue was to be 'available' to 'encourage learning' and 'to encourage parents of the need to communicate with children'. Coordinators recognised the need 'to concentrate more on home visitation'. The main focus for coordinators was the development of parents and their involvement in their children's education.

How the Coordinator Fosters Partnership

Among the sixteen principals interviewed many gave practical ways in which the coordinator fostered partnership and some spoke theoretically. We shall now review some examples from both categories. Practical examples from principals were that the coordinator was 'constantly communicating ... being positive, being open, pulling ... community and school together'. The Local Committee according to principals was a 'valiant effort to get [partnership] off the ground', where the 'parent point of view' was 'always' put forward. Principals held that 'activities and courses' run by the coordinator led in the 'long term towards partnership' while 'communication, either verbal or written', made it 'right for parents to take part'. The coordinator 'has managed to bring staff into the day-to-day running of the scheme by utilising ... people's expertise' and schools had synchronised holiday time where they served the same families. The more theoretical views of principals could be summarised as follows: that the coordinator 'communicated with teachers about the philosophy of the scheme' and that the coordinator created 'a climate where parents are genuinely seen as partners in education'.

In outlining how partnership was developed core groups said that coordinators 'had opened up the school for parents' and had provided 'classes and courses ... building up confidence and assertiveness, parenting and communication skills'. Coordinators had parents and teachers 'working together on equal terms, feeling like you're an equal with the teacher'. In the same vein, another core group said that 'partnership implies equality and in the old days the teachers were apart'. Core groups held that there was 'ease with the principals, that this is the best of all, you can say what you want to say ... the coordinator gave me the idea of how to approach the principal'. Home visitation 'by the coordinator ... to specialised houses (homes of marginalised children) to help children who have problems' were valuable according to core groups. Parents felt that 'we can discuss problems together. I love coming here. You're made feel welcome by the principal, teachers and coordinator ... activities all help partnership ... one of her strong aims [is] to get [us] to know each other'. A similar view point from another group was 'sharing my kid's behaviour patterns with the coordinator for the help of the kid. They would be able to work on it in the school and I work on it at home'. Core groups recommended the setting up of a 'parent council, parents and teachers socialising together, sitting together and enjoying it, at the museum together and a day out for parents, teachers and children once a year'.

As already outlined, one core group had difficulties with their school and its teachers and expressed the view that 'teachers are a law unto themselves'. They also repeated that 'you need an independent person when you come to school'. A further feeling in this group related to 'suspicion' about home visitation being done by the coordinator who was a teacher.

Coordinators believed that they fostered partnership when they 'treat everybody the same … giving information to whoever asks … never making people feel inferior'. A similar view from another coordinator was 'giving space to the views of parents where I can'. Coordinators believed that they should keep 'encouraging parents and teachers to work together … fostering partnership between various bodies'. This is summed up well by another coordinator, who aims at having 'as many as possible involved in the child's education and life' working together. A further coordinator believed that 'no one on [his/her] own builds partnership, but all together' in a 'non-judgemental' way. 'Partnership is about trust', one coordinator claimed.

In order to foster partnership, coordinators said that they needed to make changes in their own personal lives. One coordinator held that 'teachers have an elevated status' and that 'partnership involves taking a step back from that'. She believed that 'the weaker party has to be trained through a process of empowerment' because 'handing over equal decision making involves a huge change'.

Coordinators promoted joint policy making through Parents and Teachers Working Together on Policy Formation. They encouraged 'outreach meetings' in order 'to prevent early school leaving'. They have 'people listening to one another in a very active way, trying to understand where the other is coming from' and then seeking 'to marry the understanding and the communication'.

According to coordinators, they focused on the 'new parent-teacher meetings' where parents discussed their hopes and concerns for their children in small groups, suggested a suitable amount of homework, appropriate pupil behaviour and outlined how the school might help parents through the person of the coordinator. This was reiterated by another coordinator whose constant question to parents was 'are needs being met?' and by still another who 'never made plans around parents behind their backs'. Coordinators held Local Committee meetings 'on a regular basis' where 'principals, parents and local agencies meet on different issues' such as school 'attendance', 'after school activities', 'making the school more user friendly' and 'the motivation of students'. Coordinators 'constantly involve parents, teachers and students' together in 'supervised study' or through 'care teams' within the school.

How the HSCL Scheme Could be Improved

All interviewees were asked for their 'ideas' on how the HSCL Scheme could be improved. There were two reasons for this request. Firstly, so that shortcomings in the current situation could be deduced and secondly, to anticipate, to determine the way forward, allowing prevalent needs and practice to inform the theory of HSCL. We recall the words of W. Burkan, a professional trainer whose clients include Motorola, that 'organizational change must be led top-down but must be engineered bottom-up'.[59] This was Department of Education theory and it has informed the HSCL Scheme since its inception in 1990.

The recommendations, for the future development of the HSCL Scheme, from principals included the following: the provision of 'in-career development for teachers' as a 'module on summer courses' or as a 'week in the summer for teachers, a conference'. This is a time when 'class teachers and coordinator would be more involved in planning together'. Another was the inclusion of HSCL theory as 'modules in teacher training colleges'. Other recommendations related to resources such as the appointment of more HSCL coordinators to allow one school per coordinator, of more teachers of remedial education, of child care workers and of a secretary for the coordinator. The distribution of more finance to coordinators was also named. Principals claimed that there was a need for the encouragement/inclusion of 'more parents', better 'attendance at parent-teacher meetings', of more 'involvement of staff' and more 'home visits' as coordinators are 'still not reaching the uninvolved'. Principals said that coordinators sought to protect the fact that all are involved in making the school 'the best possible place for children' and that all 'work together, really, instead of against each other'.

Only one of the fifteen principals interviewed could see the role of coordinator being filled by anyone other than a teacher. That particular principal said that a local mother could fulfil the role 'if she came in through the HSCL Scheme with the coordinator'. The other fourteen principals held that a non-teacher 'wouldn't be accepted from the point of view of staff', 'wouldn't be as effective', would be more threatening 'for the most needy people', would require 'qualification or credentials', and qualities such as 'sympathy, understanding, psychology training, discretion, confidentiality and sensitivity'.

Recommendations for improving the HSCL Scheme, according to core groups were 'to expand' the scheme and 'to make it better' by providing more 'coordinators', 'more money', 'a secretary for the coordinator' and 'more publicity about HSCL from the school'. Core groups recommended that the services to schools of 'school books at post-primary level', of 'computers' and of 'swimming classes out of school hours' should be extended. Parents believed that 'talks on drugs from parents' for parents, a 'counselling service' for pupils and families and the maintaining of 'the community aspect of the HSCL Scheme' should be developed. Parents also felt that administration issues such as better heat, access to the building, safety in the building and environs and respect for the basic needs of children should be promoted. To ensure anonymity, specific examples are not given here in this text, but were given at interview.

Ten core groups maintained that it was an 'advantage to have an experience of teaching' for the role of coordinator while four groups claimed that someone from the community 'could be trained' if 'you have children and are around forty'. One core group held that 'you need an independent person' from 'the area', who has 'more in common with parents' and does not 'go at four p.m.', someone for whom the principal is not 'the boss'.

The coordinators, in their recommendations, suggested the team approach through a 'network of parents', a 'network of principals' and through coordinators 'working as a local team … operating like a huge Local Committee' working in 'each others' schools'. Coordinators also recommended 'better cooperation from within the staff' with 'time for staffs to work on and focus on issues of home and school … staff need to work on their own, and then come together' with parents. 'Parents and staff could set up programmes for children during summer months' they suggested. A further point relating to staff was to broaden the coordinator's role with teachers to include 'new ways of looking at curriculum and instruction'. Setting 'a precedent of six years' on the length of time a teacher spends in the role of HSCL coordinator would improve matters. This would spread the interest in the role throughout the staff and ensure more first-hand experience of liaison.

Extending the National Coordinator services so the local coordinators could have 'more visits on the ground' would improve the HSCL Scheme, according to some coordinators.

Of the eighteen coordinators interviewed, one claimed that 'a dynamic person [parent] with training' could do the role of coordinating, but that 'at this point it would be inconceivable'. Seven other coordinators agreed it could be someone other than a teacher, but in each case qualified their view with 'I don't think it would be ideal', or 'the teachers trust me' as a colleague, or 'it makes a huge difference to have a teacher'.

Fourteen of the sixteen chairpersons circularised had ideas about how the HSCL Scheme 'could be improved'. They claimed that improved 'staffing and funding' to the school would make a difference (31 per cent). An 'awareness in the community' (27.6 per cent), an 'awareness' among staff members (20.7 per cent) ' together with an awareness on BOM' (6.9 per cent) could improve scheme functioning.' Chairpersons also held that a policy on HSCL' (6.9 per cent) could improve scheme practices. The remainder, 6.9 per cent of chairpersons, were satisfied with the scheme as it was.[60]

Outcomes from Questionnaires Sent to Individual Parents of the Sixteen Selected Schools

Throughout the interviews we have been examining the perception of the coordinator by principals, core groups of parents and the coordinator's own evaluation. We have explored the values and beliefs that the coordinator holds, how coordinators develop a sense of team, interrelatedness and partnership, in short, if and how the coordinator performed as leader. The interviews were valuable in that they authenticated the positive evaluation of coordinators by themselves and by others.

Since the 'core groups' of parents interviewed were in all cases parents who had involved themselves closely with the work of the coordinator, it was decided to acquire information from another cohort of parents. A questionnaire was sent to a representative sample of parents in the sixteen schools selected for an indepth study. A total of 123 parents were circularised. The response rate was 93.5 per cent. Just over half of the questionnaire was directly associated with the role of the coordinator and sought similar information to that pursued in the interviews. Parents were given statements and asked to tick 'which expresses your views in relation to this school'. Statements given to parents which were directly related to the work of the coordinator are in the Table 4.2.

Among these randomly selected parents 73.9 per cent felt they knew the coordinator 'very well' and 73 per cent considered him/her as 'a friend' while 69.6 per cent got 'a lot of news' from the coordinator. From the foregoing we can deduce that the coordinators' communication ability seems high and their acceptance by parents was likewise.

Just 33.9 per cent of the parents went to the parents' room and only 23.5 per cent had done a course/courses in the previous year. Of the percentage who did courses, 5.2 per cent did not attend the parents' room. Of the 115 parents who returned questionnaires, 39.1 per cent met the coordinator in the parents' room or at courses. While this percentage is very hopeful, there is still a large number of parents in the 'no opinion/strongly disagree/disagree' categories in Table 4.2.

Regarding contact with the coordinator through home visitation, 60 per cent of parents liked the coordinator to visit them in their own home. Just under half of these parents either attended in the parents' room or did a course/courses, while for the other half, home visitation was the only contact between the parent and the coordinator. Of the 115 parents who responded 70 per cent met the coordinator in at least one of the following locations: the parents' room, at courses, or during home

Table 4.2 Responses from Individual Parents Regarding the Coordinator's Work

Statement	Strongly Agree	Agree	No opinion	Disagree	Strongly Disagree	Yes	No	No reply
I know the Home/School Teacher (Coordinator) very well	25.2	48.7	13.0	11.3	1.7	n/a	n/a	0.0
I get a lot of news from the Home/School Teacher (Coordinator)	18.3	51.3	13.0	13.9	1.7	n/a	n/a	1.7
I feel that I have a friend in the Home/School Teacher (Coordinator)	21.7	51.3	15.7	10.4	0.9	n/a	n/a	0.0
I have got great confidence from working with the Home/School Teacher (Coordinator)	22.6	38.3	27.8	9.6	0.9	n/a	n/a	0.9
I feel the benefit of working with the Home/School Teacher (Coordinator) when I am at home with my child/children	13.0	41.7	32.2	9.6	1.7	n/a	n/a	1.7
I go to the Parents' Room in the school	n/a	n/a	n/a	n/a	n/a	33.9	64.3	1.7
Spending time in the Parents' Room is helpful to me as a parent.	n/a	n/a	n/a	n/a	n/a	33.9	8.7	57.4
Last year I did a course/courses in this school.	n/a	n/a	n/a	n/a	n/a	23.5	64.3	12.2
I like the Home/School teacher (Coordinator) to visit me in my home.	n/a	n/a	n/a	n/a	n/a	60.0	35.7	4.3

[Percentages rounded up/down to 0.1 per cent]

visitation. This finding in itself seems very positive. It should also be acknowledged that home visitation could have taken place with the 35.7 per cent who did not like the coordinator to visit them at home and the 4.3 per cent who did not comment. However, if this is the case parents have never voiced their disapproval to the coordinators. It could also be a fact that those who did not have a home visit were among the middle income sector of the post-primary school and not within the brief of the coordinator. Some gains accepted by parents, from working with the coordinators, were 'great confidence' (60.9 per cent) and 'benefit' when at home with children (54.7 per cent).

Within the sixteen randomly selected schools, one primary school and three of the schools at post-primary level have a middle-income sector for which the coordinator does not have responsibility. This could account for some of the parents who have not attended in the parents' room or at courses. It could also be part of the reason why 40 per cent of parents may not have had a home visit.

Conclusion

The interviews were an obvious and necessary piece of research as it allowed for a cross-check on the research findings.[61] Being qualitative research and interview it allowed people to be more at ease and to mention the things both positive, and negative, that may not have emerged in the questionnaire. The author as interviewer completed the interviews. It is perhaps important to note that at the time of interview and immediately before, the author had done substantial analysis on the questionnaires and was therefore very alert either to confirmation or negation of the main questionnaire findings.

The interviews did not give evidence of negative elements that had not already surfaced in the questionnaires. One result of the interviews, which is not susceptible to scientific quantification, is the warmth and enthusiasm of others for the coordinators. The author would have been slow to speak so eagerly about the coordinators merely on the basis of the questionnaire, but the interviews have done it in a different way. Likewise, one can see a sense of personal commitment, fulfilment and professional satisfaction on the part of the coordinators themselves.

All this being said, the interviews, despite recording a strong positive appreciation of the HSCL Scheme and particularly of the coordinators, are not starry-eyed – whilst recognising achievement, everybody involved acknowledges that much more needs to be done. Home visitation is not fully implemented, but the interviews show how much appreciated it is by parents. Theoretical worries about home visitation that it might for instance be regarded as intrusive, particularly in low-income families, are not borne out by the interviews.

Another issue that one might wonder about, namely, whether the coordinators might be other than a teacher seems decisively answered on the part of parents, who value what is probably a combination of the status, professionalism and experience of the coordinator. It was similarly responded to by the coordinators themselves, who sense that acceptance on the part of other teachers and perhaps the principals is to a large extent conditional on the coordinator being a teacher. A lot of the coordinator skills such as partnership, listening and HSCL philosophy could be taught to open minded parents, and it is hard to see why familiarity with curriculum and the actual tensions of the classroom, which a teacher brings to the job, should somehow be an essential element in the coordinator's background.

CHAPTER FIVE

Practical Steps

IN MODERN TIMES structures that are human, focused and task driven enable people to perform well in the workplace and to be more content at work. Groups committed to change and transformation need to build 'supportive structures and patterns of working with people that are consistent with their overall aims'.[1] There are three aspects to an organisation 'the formal structure, which can be shown on an organization chart; there are policies and procedures; and, more important than these two, there is people's behaviour within the organization'.[2]

While the foregoing comments refer to any group or organisation, they also hold true for schools. In *Changing Teachers, Changing Times*, A. Hargreaves, Professor of Educational Administration in Ontario, tells us that in any talk about schooling, corporate analogies are common, yet they are also contested.

> Schools are not businesses. Children are not products ... Schools and corporations, however, are not absolutely unalike ... When the corporate world encounters major crises and undergoes profound transitions, human service organizations like hospitals and schools should pay close attention, for similar crises may soon affect them.[3]

Irish Department of Education policy, which is reflected in 'Charting our Education Future', presents the argument that

> Schools, in common with most organisations, can derive many benefits from engaging in a systematic planning process. This process of planning offers an excellent opportunity for engaging the board of management, the principal, staff and parents in a collaborative exercise aimed at defining the school's mission and putting in place policies which will determine the activities of the school.[4]

It is widely held in literature on education today, that structures are required that will provide the school community with:

- a clear sense of *purpose*, why the school exists
- a *value* system, what the school believes in
- a *vision statement*, what the school could become
- a *mission statement*, the path the school follows
- named *goals*, clearly stated, time related and achievable
- defined *objectives*, statements based on end results
- *role identification* procedures, clarification of roles with their inherent rights and responsibilities
- a high level of *organisation*, who will do what, why, when, where, how, by when
- an *implementation* stage, focus on tasks, targets and monitoring
- on-going *feedback, evaluation, delegation*
- a deep sense of the *value of people* both as participants and beneficiaries.

The last point, referring to mutual respect, is coloured very much by the ethos-school culture and this ethos-school culture is enhanced by the level of respect people have for one another.[5]

Structure

We shall examine the term structure from various standpoints.

> The structure of an organisation, of a school, defines the shape of organisation and the roles within it ... the rules, procedures and policies the group adopts for its operations are also laid down in the organisational structure ... without structures it is often unclear who does what, and without a structured approach to participation, many voices can go unheard.[6]

In addition to a structured approach to planning and evaluation – the task completion aspect – there is need also for structures that are human and caring. A human, caring structure draws on the innate goodness in every human person and allows that goodness to flourish and grow for the benefit of all in the school. K. Blanchard, who is involved in training and development, and M. O'Connor, a 'master' in behavioural research, put it succinctly: 'there's something good in people that is brought out when they pool their energies to serve something bigger'.[7]

Structures within the school community should enable individuals and the group as a whole to develop their strengths, to reduce the negative consequences of personal limitation, to build a system of accountability, to maintain commitment, to support one another and to fulfil their role purposefully and as effectively as possible.

Sense of Purpose

What do we mean by a clear sense of *purpose*? Effective work starts with a clear purpose that in some way incorporates the hoped-for outcomes. Again, Blanchard and others believe that it is through 'empowerment, relationships and communication, flexibility and recognition and appreciation' that the hoped-for outcome is reached.[8] These authors relate a simple story of two workers hammering on a piece of granite. When asked what they were doing, one worker said, 'I'm trying to crack this granite', the other responded 'I'm part of a team building a cathedral'.[9] In the school context, G. Pugh of the National Children's Bureau in London, speaks of partnership between home and school as a working relationship characterised by 'a shared sense of purpose'.[10] With S. Clayton, a theorist on team development and supervision, we can say 'purpose is the passion that drives people and organizations forward'.[11] Statements of purpose can be understood in terms of values and values can be expressed in the language of purpose.

Value System

At the heart of a school, or indeed any organisation, lies a set of *values*, which school personnel may or may not subscribe to. Clayton states that 'when the majority of the people fully subscribe to these values ... then the organisation has a growing heart. People feel good because they can be authentic. People are able to learn and take risks. Creativity and innovation permeate the culture ... The open hearted organisation will carry a collective sense of purpose'.[12] So schools must enunciate and encourage commitment to core values concerned with the quality of life and relationships within the school community. A value system provides 'a sense of direction, shared values can help people to see beyond immediate clashes of interest and act on behalf of a larger, long-term, mutual interest'.[13] J. Adair, a British writer on organisational issues, particularly in the area of time management, believes that values are 'essentially what you think is worthwhile and deserving of effort'.[14] He acknowledges 'a reverse effect ... by choosing an object and devoting ourselves to it, we create value'.[15] S. Covey and A. Merrill, writing on effectiveness, hold that 'to value something is to esteem it to be of worth ... critically important', but they also state that valuing something 'does not necessarily mean it will create quality-of-life results'.[16] Hence, there is a need to take time to clarify the values, and to work towards consensus where possible, while recognising differences. In this way 'shared values can become the basis for decision-making'.[17] These authors also hold that 'the real "boss" is the company's adopted values'.[18] The value system, they believe, is 'the authority we must serve'.[19]

This notion of service being a value in itself is found in modern literature. In *Stewardship*, Block has *Choosing Service over Self-Interest* as the subtitle. He defines partnership as the willingness 'to give more choice to the people we choose to serve'.[20] The authors of *Managing by Values* believe that 'success ... is all about service ... and service means people ... As a result of aligning with and living by ones values, we've seen decreases in legal costs ... complaints ... wage disputes ... in locations where there's been a significant recession'.[21] A former Harvard Professor, D. H. Maister, holds the view that 'schools and firms should find ways to teach more about what it is to serve'.[22] Later on he links the notion of service and value. He speaks of asking people 'how to serve them better', he speaks of listening to them, 'demonstrating an interest' in them, and offering 'something of value' to them.[23]

So we can conclude that values are at the centre of our actions individually and collectively and underpin the work of the school. 'Schools need to devote both time and preparation to this, as the aim is to end with a set of core values that everyone in the school understands and can support ... At the very least all the staff should play an active part, and at best all the children and their parents will also be involved'.[24] The education of the whole child within the context of a whole-school approach requires an integrated value system where faith, truth, respect, love, justice, learning, freedom and tolerance abound.[25] The value system underpins the work and the culture of the school.

Having a Clear Vision

Now we turn to the concept of *vision*. J. Harvey-Jones, a well known British businessman speaks of vision as the creation of a 'better world', a creation by the leader, of 'a dream for the business – and more particularly for the people in it ... it has to be owned by others'.[26]

The words of Harvey-Jones can easily be applied to the school situation. Reluctance to articulate a vision can stem from fear of change, a lack of hope, or a hesitancy to take responsibility for our own lives. A vision statement 'is an expression of hope, and if we have no hope, it is hard to create a vision'.[27] The challenge is to pursue our vision with 'as much courage and intensity as we can generate. Change takes place slowly inside each of us and by the choices we think through'.[28] Change means abandoning the security and predictability of the present that we have learned to adjust to. It means acquiring new skills, forming new relationships and devising new patterns of working with which we are unfamiliar.

'The greatest risk of all is making no change, because it is inevitable that others will overtake you'.[29] Part of the vision-change-vision movement is 'to know how to learn from the future'.[30] This sense of future vision that permeates the writing of V. Frankl, a psychologist who survived Auschwitz, is probably one of the most needed qualities in the early years of the twenty-first century.[31] Teachers who can make the shift from being teacher to being educator will inevitably move from being expert to agent. This vision of their role will also enable them to be 'counsellor and facilitator, manager of learning situations, coordinator of projects, team leader or network resource'.[32] Teachers often place limitations on what they allow themselves to imagine. This curtails the range of possibilities available, and curtails the turning of dreams into visions, 'far fewer still will persevere through the drudgery of sustaining the vision'.[33] A value system guides the behaviour people should use to achieve change. Schools that 'excel at change work hard at the values level'.[34] We sum up this section on vision in the words of A. Leith and M. Maynard, consultants and team trainers, who provide an implementation and development process for vision:

- express the vision
- behave in ways, which advance the goal of making it happen
- explain the vision so people know what is required in terms of specific action
- extend the vision, applying it to various situations
- expand the vision, using it in many different ways, in a wide range of circumstances.[35]

The above process presumes that the vision has been shared and owned by the entire group, school, or organisation. When employees have a sense of ownership of the vision they will feel 'more confident and more "empowered" to take decisions which are consistent with the organisation's overall purpose, aims and objectives'.[36] The vision is the distant picture of the place we are heading for. We need to believe in it, communicate it, live by it, and feel for it with real passion. There is a wide body of research evidence, which indicates that every leader, indeed every individual, needs to articulate a 'vision of greatness'.[37] It is widely held that a vision can only inspire and energise people and attract commitment '[when] it offers a view of the future that is clearly and demonstrably better for the organization, for the people in the organization, and/or for the society within which the organization operates ... a bold and worthy challenge for those who accept it'.[38] According to J. A. Belasco, a professor of Management in San Diego, the vision needs to be shared, it 'specifies a mutual destination, the place everyone agrees to go, and the major activities that get you there'.[39] Again from the same author we hear that people 'can only be empowered by a vision they understand'.[40]

The Mission – the Path the School Follows

The *mission* of the school guides staff in their work in the present, it is not a vision of the future although it contains the vision within it. The mission of the school is the path the school follows, a path that will add value to the school. This path defines the 'purpose, the business, the philosophy, the culture ... people's values and beliefs, their enthusiasm and pride'.[41] Furthermore P. Dobson and K. Starkey, lecturers in the University of Nottingham, hold that a mission statement defines 'the code of conduct that tells employees how to behave'.[42]

Naming Goals

Naming *goals*, establishing priorities, helps the individual and the group, the teacher and the school, to structure action so as 'to avoid aimless or undirected activity'.[43] Goals help to make the vision a reality. Goals need to be clearly stated; 'this brings authority, accountability and permanence to your priorities'.[44] Goals should be aspirational but time related, that is, realisable within the time frame of a given plan. 'Successful people set goals that are ambitious yet realistic'.[45] Working towards the realisation of goals means being responsible to people. Accountability for the use of our time is critical, without it 'goals melt away forgotten'.[46]

Objectives

Goals must be distinguished from *objectives* 'which need to be achieved on the way to the goals'.[47] Having said that, goals and objectives are often used interchangeably in the literature. S. Costello, a private consultant specialising in management training, is very clear that objectives are statements based on outputs or end results – 'always write objectives in terms of end results not in terms of activities'.[48] To realise objectives 'there need to be policies – the ways in which the objectives are to be attained'.[49]

The literature on management, both for business and for school, is strong in its emphasis on the involvement of people in designing the plans and processes for use in their establishment. It is equally strong in the sense of 'ownership' required before plans will be implemented. According to L. Bell, a British researcher, 'giving more responsibility, a more interesting activity, freedom to plan and implement … providing more opportunity to express a particular talent' supplies opportunities to manage a team 'to obtain the best effect' while also 'achieving team objectives'.[50]

Role Identification, Rights and Responsibilities

One of the most common causes of misunderstanding and friction between individuals and groups is the lack of clarity around *roles* and the inherent *rights* and *responsibilities* that accompany those roles. There can be blame, jealousy regarding strengths and abilities, confusion, tension and apathy where working expectations are unclear. Where employers view people as 'employees' rather than as partners in the enterprise they deny them responsibility, the freedom to be flexible and the 'opportunities to learn and to use what they learn', in short, they deny them basic rights.[51]

Within the workplace people have a right to expect and to receive 'understanding, if a request of them is unreasonable or prejudicial to their personal beliefs or needs, support to fulfil corporate or department objectives, honest, ethical, moral and legal conduct from colleagues and superiors'.[52] In relation to pupils, J. Ungoed-Thomas, a former member of HM Inspectorate, holds that the right to liberty 'includes the educationally vital right as to what sort of person one desires to become'.[53] Generally, the employee horizon is limited by leadership/management if roles have not been clarified. However when strengths have been identified and roles clarified, firms, organisations and schools can 'ally themselves ... in order to gain specialised expertise'.[54] The cost of developing expertise independently can be 'simply prohibitive'.[55] Inspiring individual and corporate initiatives requires that leaders and followers accept responsibility to and through what they do. The rights mentioned above are balanced by responsibilities, which include 'being available, approachable and responsive, listening ... sharing, decision-making ... providing information, being aware of others' personal beliefs ... honouring these responsibilities by being consciously aware of other people'.[56]

The Organisation and Implementation Stages

More detailed work on roles takes place as we progress through the *organisation* stage. At this level we deal with vital questions such as who will do what, why, when, where, how, by when etc. Many programmes do not reach the desired outcome because the organisation stage does not receive the necessary attention. Programme planning requires a deep understanding of people and of their real needs. In addition, those who ask the basic questions 'what will we do?' and 'why will we do it?' need to be able to develop programmes, materials, and ways of working that will respond to the deep-seated needs and desires of the people concerned.

The success of the *implementation* stage depends very much on the quality of all the preceding steps. An ability to name and share the vision, to state clear goals, to define objectives, to access clarity around roles, rights and responsibilities and to develop a high level of organisation creates a readiness 'to begin implementing plans in a truly organised way'.[57] D. Dorr, a researcher for Saint Patrick's Missionary Society, claims that

> Almost as soon as a movement begins to implement a planned programme, its members are choosing to move in one of two very different directions. Either they are acting in such a way that the curve of life, hope, and expansion continues to rise, or their approach is one that causes the movement to begin to slide down the curve of death.[58]

A sense of ownership of the plan being implemented is vital, so also is the well-being of the people concerned, for

> even the most innovative strategy will not work if people are not committed and involved in the implementation process ... without the guidelines and framework of sound strategies and continuous development of human resources as the most important asset, one may exert only modest returns.[59]

Feedback and *evaluation* are intertwined and interdependent. Feedback, if graciously received, enables the individual and the team 'to step back and look at how they are reaching their goals ... and redesign their ways of working ... [it is] a continuous process ... a great discovery of the quality programme is often that the people who are doing a task are the best people to redesign it'.[60] Evaluation is 'also a matter of dreaming dreams, of using imagination, of inspiration and insight'.[61] The opposite may hold when organisations and individuals 'refuse to recognize the reality of their present situation'.[62] J.P. Kotter of Harvard Business School believed that 'even in a rapidly changing world, someone has to make the current system perform to expectation ... if short-term wins don't demonstrate that you're on the right path, you will rarely get the chance to fully implement your vision'.[63] Dobson and Starkey held a similar view and stated 'when vigilance and evaluation suggest that the objectives of the business or the major plans and policies are no longer appropriate, or that the results of implementing the strategy do not confirm their cultural assumptions, then it is time to change'.[64]

Feedback, Evaluation and Delegation

Through constructive feedback people learn about themselves and the effect they have on others. 'Constructive feedback can increase self-awareness and offer ideas to encourage development'.[65] Constructive feedback can be either positive or negative. However, 'negative feedback, if given sensitively and skilfully, is just as important to self-development'.[66] Modern literature on management emphasises the importance of listing people's strengths first, and secondly, looking at what could be improved. Feedback is an 'inseparable part of interpersonal and inter-team communication'.[67] Work groups with this type of rapport have 'open, empathic, solution-oriented communication'. Group members talk openly with one another and with their managers and are open to giving and receiving feedback'.[68] W.A. Pasmore, a management consultant, believed that 'people want to know how they have done individually, as a team, as a unit, as an organization' and that 'when feedback was improved, it never caused performance to decline'.[69] J. MacBeath proposes the 'critical friend' as the 'successful marrying of unconditional support and unconditional critique'.[70] Feedback processes, according to R. Halsall, a researcher in Manchester, 'are the mechanisms by which culture and values are maintained and challenged'.[71] Good communication/consultation/feedback lead to team reviews and more formal evaluation structures. According to Leigh and Maynard, team reviews

> identify blocks to team working, resolve interpersonal problems, give the team fresh momentum, provide new direction, keep the team fresh, inspire people, improve commitment, help understand what is happening, revise a thirst for growth and change, restimulate a hunger for the next big target refocus attention on the big (strategic) picture.[72]

Feedback should be 'specific ... factual ... not emotional ... directly work related ... constructive ... relevant to behaviour not personality'.[73] For T. Russell, a consultant working in London and Australia, a definite feedback formula should be used. A formula where people 'can see what they have done ... the effect of their behaviour [and] "agree" a change'.[74] When feedback is genuinely given it is usually well received and it makes the evaluation process much more achievable. The trust that is built in the process creates the possibility for delegation. Feedback processes enable the hearing of the views of others and the hearing of the response. They are also the means whereby the ethos, value system and vision of the school can be 'maintained and challenged'.[75]

The *delegation* process provides new challenges for those who have reached the team level and enables those who have too much to do to seek different challenges.[76] Some criteria are essential in order to delegate effectively:

- analysing your own job – 'which things must you personally do?'[77]
- correctly identifying 'the person to whom work is being delegated – are they capable? Are they willing?'[78]
- creating 'a common purpose that people can share and ensuring that they understand this clearly'[79]
- briefing and coaching of personnel
- monitoring how personnel are getting on while learning to trust them
- being available if required
- reviewing what has been learned.

The delegation process promotes a sense of being valued. Delegation means giving people more control. 'People are allowed more freedom of action within specified limits … holding them accountable for the results'.[80]

Investment in People and Leadership

People are our most important asset. These words appear in reports, they are verbalised at meetings and seminars and they abound in the literature delineating leadership in schools and in other influential organisations. There needs to be a deep sense of the *value of people* both as participants and beneficiaries. Valuing people brings with it 'noticeable gains on a variety of levels'.[81] Enhancing interpersonal relationships has 'benefits for you personally and professionally, there are benefits for your staff personally and professionally, there are benefits for the whole team, and there are benefits for the organization'.[82] S. Cane, a British industrialist, puts the valuing of people succinctly when she says 'only organisations that place as much priority on their human resource strategy as their business strategy will have the strength to become and remain first class'.[83]

Leadership is about demonstrating belief in people, providing support and challenging them. It is 'giving people the capability to inspire themselves – not creating followers, but other leaders throughout the organization'.[84] K. Ohmae, a Japanese business strategist, believes that 'When companies talk about ensuring employee participation and contributing to their people's well-being ... it is strong evidence that their value systems and whole management processes are really built around people'.[85] He continues to speak about the value of 'people who can think strategically', people who possess 'sensitivity, insight and an inquisitive mind', in short, people who can challenge the 'status quo'.[86] Successful people share the profound urge to strive, to make progress, to achieve their goals and to fulfil the vision of the organisation, of the school. A leader in organisational communication, P. Stoltz, who had among his clients Deloitte & Touche and Motorola, puts it this way:

> Climbers embrace challenges and they live with a sense of urgency. They are self-motivated, highly driven, and strive to get the utmost out of life ... Climbers work with vision ... They thrive on the challenge ... you can count on (them) to make things happen.[87]

The self-motivated, highly enthusiastic and happy worker outlined by Stoltz, more than likely belongs to a learning organisation where 'school-based studies' are 'part of a never-ending extension of the professionalism of the people concerned', and where development is 'embedded in the value system of the institution'.[88] Burkan would add that this type of institution has not just a past and a present focus, but an ability to 'learn from the future',[89] while C. Handy, a visiting professor to the London Business School 'is more and more sure that those who are in love with learning are in love with life'.[90] In developing the quality of the professional, Maister urges that organisations should invest in the development of people, use modern technique and technology and provide emotional support.[91]

Through a helpful and constructive approach people learn to believe in themselves, and can enjoy greater happiness and success at work. This proactive approach can lead to better job performance for the individual concerned and frequently 'other members of the organization operate differently'.[92] A. Dubrin, from the Rochester Institute in New York, holds that 'Success stories are a natural way of inspiring others to extend themselves'.[93]

D. Buchanan and A. Huczynski, organisational behaviourists in Leicester and Glasgow, debate the values of both the human and the structural approaches. They assert that social scientists see the individual as playing a minor role and that behaviour is determined by the organisational structure. It is their belief that those coming from a management perspective tend to focus on individual and group characteristics.[94] No doubt the truth – the reality – lies in blending both approaches. Too many groups fail to maximise potential 'because they consider their business strategy in isolation. It is therefore essential that an organization's overall strategy is linked from the very beginning to its human resource strategy'.[95] Handy is aligned with Cane in his view that while the trend in organisations had been 'to play down the importance of the individual and the group leader' in favour of 'structure, control systems and climate', the tide has now turned to favour 'the importance of the individual'.[96] M.G. McIntyre, a consultant from Atlanta, claims that social activities and 'having fun as a group is an important part of team maintenance'.[97] Humour helps 'to build relationships, improve communication and reduce tensions'.[98]

Communication

There is much emphasis today, in theory and in practice, on the value of active listening leading to good communication. A recent poll of top managers in American corporations named 'the ability to express oneself clearly and forcefully' as the main quality they looked for in young graduates.[99] Iacocca believed that management is about motivating other people and that 'the only way you can motivate people is to communicate with them. You may know your subject, but you have to keep in mind that your audience is coming in cold ... a good manager needs to listen at least as much as he needs to talk ... real communication goes in both directions'.[100] Of the same opinion is P. Lagadec, a research scientist in the area of crisis management in Paris, who says that 'communicating does not simply mean being able to send messages, it also means being able to receive them'.[101]

Cane, speaking about the traditional downward communication, emphasises the need for 'upward and cross-functional communication'.[102] She claims that effective communication presupposes an equality and respect between the parties to ensure clear reception in which it is 'just as important to listen as to speak'.[103] Implicit in the Kaizen method (a Japanese form of leadership that places no emphasis on aims for 'perfection' or reaching 'targets', as they are limiting, but rather outputs referred to as 'standards') is the practice of 'inter-departmental or cross-functional co-operation'.[104] This method of inter-departmental cooperation – the readiness to work with other agencies and departments – has been one of the Basic Principles of the HSCL Scheme since its inception. It has been further elucidated when speaking on 'networking' and the 'integrated delivery of service', in Chapter Three.

A good communication method calls for clarity on the part of the person delivering the message. It also requires that the deliverer has a clear understanding of the audience and its interests. Added to the foregoing requirements is the need to discern just what information the audience requires. Finally, the deliverer needs to decide on the method for use. P. Wellington, who works in the field of consultancy, encapsulates this in her eight purposes for communicating: 'to inform, to reinforce understanding, to engender openness, to promote involvement, to motivate, to enable, to reinforce personal identity with a work team, the company and its mission, and to maintain focus on customer satisfaction'.[105]

On an individual basis, communication is about paying attention, affirming, bonding, influencing and encouraging a sense of responsibility. Within teams and groups, communication meets a number of fundamental needs. In a number of both formal and informal ways communication 'assists the process of gelling ... helps clarify the purpose and aims ... is the means by which expectations and standards are established, strengthens group or team identity ... strengthens individual identity and acceptance'.[106] Communication occurs when someone reacts to the communicator. Communication, however, seeks more, namely to influence a response.

In the communication-process in schools, involving homes and the local community, it is important to remember that a frequent barrier to effective communication and to influencing people is overload. R. Hale and P. Whitlam, European business consultants, hold 'that the reason a person is selective in their listening is due to the sheer amount of information coming at them'.[107] G. Johnson and K. Scholes, both professors of strategic management in Britain, calling for 'clarity of communication' and for delivery of 'no more than three strategic messages' seem to hold the same viewpoint.[108]

Consulting people involves two-way communication, inviting people to share their views and to ask questions. There may or may not be an intention to act on the opinions expressed 'two-way communication involves more than consultation. It includes encouraging people to make suggestions'.[109] Business companies and school staffs need to invest in developing the expertise of their people. They need to establish 'the tools, processes and relationships' necessary to encourage and support 'horizontal flows of information' and the 'lateral sharing of knowledge'.[110] The outcome from a communication-consultation process can be the building of a 'strong sense of trust, both among colleagues and between superiors and subordinates'.[111]

People like and value individual attention. Such attention is required more often than people admit.[112] For T. Barnes, trained in Japan and working in human resource programmes throughout the Pacific Basin and in Britain, there are five components in interpersonal relationships and they are 'communication, training, motivation, empowerment and reward'.[113] He speaks of Kaizen leaders who act as 'communication gatekeepers'.[114] In such organisations they are answerable for 'the free flow of communication, responsible for originating, receiving, interpreting, presenting, channelling and managing information.'[115]

B. Nanus, an independent leadership consultant at the University of Southern California, speaks of communication as a 'simple dialogue' where the leader listens 'sympathetically' to the worker 'sensing' the desire to help, putting 'concerns into a larger context' while sending the worker off 'to solve the problems'.[116] During this 'simple dialogue' process P. Senge, director of the Centre of Organisational Learning in London, and his colleagues, believe that 'people learn how to think together'.[117] The sense of responsibility in solving ones own problems, referred to by Nanus above, 'calls for highly developed communication and influence skills' according to E. Zuker, a trainer and management consultant in San Francisco.[118]

Frequently, due to a limited flow of information people can hold a private interpretation of the other's intent, which can lead to 'a mutual undermining of relationship'.[119] This conflict is an outcome of 'distorted communication' and can influence many.[120] Another factor that interferes with the communication process is the inability to keep abreast of changes and growth within groups, the inability to update communication methods. J.F. Benson, a psychotherapist and teacher in Belfast, claims 'that methods of communication which were acceptable at earlier stages of development need reworking ... because the emergence of more sophisticated collaborative activity requires a corresponding evolution'.[121]

H. Telford, a primary and post-primary teacher and head, also lecturing at the University of Melbourne, examined leadership in urban schools through a 'structural frame' and through a 'human resource frame' in order 'to achieve success for students'.[122] She built her 'human resource frame' on the fundamental premise 'that the individual talents, skill and energy of the people in an organization are its most vital resource'.[123] Leigh and Maynard held similar views, and claimed that one of the ways 'to unlock potential' is by 'valuing people'.[124] They gave a number of prescriptions if 'valuing' is to happen: 'provide a worthwhile role ... recognise peoples' efforts ... listen to people carefully ... speak to people with respect ... discover how people are feeling ... express concern about their welfare ... ensure their work is valued by others'.[125]

The Teaching-Learning Environment and the Child

In the presence of groups of teachers one will note how action-orientated they are and how much they seek practical ideas. Teachers are faced with many pressures, new curricula and approaches to evaluation, pupils who bring a diversity of backgrounds, who have different learning needs, abilities and attitudes to learning, and demands from parents and the wider community. It is often 'easier to do what you have always done ... than develop new strategies or evaluate current ones'.[126] Classroom and school evaluation 'is a meaningful activity that engages teachers in a process of refinement, helps create autonomy in professional judgement and enhances practice'.[127] When teachers are involved in classroom and school improvement they become part of a 'learning community'.[128] In this way teachers contribute to their own learning and the learning of others.[129]

The purpose of school development is to improve the quality of teaching and learning in the classroom 'through the successful management of innovation and change'.[130] School development calls for change in the culture and structures of schooling 'reinvented for and realigned with the post-modern purposes and pressures they must now address'.[131] To be in a position to implement the vision, goal and objectives of the school, teachers require 'systematic and carefully considered support'.[132] M. Fullan, an innovator and leader in teacher education in Toronto, and A. Hargreaves, professor of educational administration in Ontario, call for 'a particular culture of teaching', a set of working relationships that bind teachers together 'in a supportive, inquiring community ... in schools which value, develop and support the judgement and expertise of all their teachers'.[133]

The teacher as 'career-long learner' is central to the growth and development of the pupils.[134] Block encourages people to 'learn as much as you can about what you're doing. Learning and performance are intimately related'.[135] Teacher development and pupil development are closely linked as Fullan and Hargreaves point out 'the value of teacher development and teacher collaboration must ultimately be judged by whether these changes make teachers better for their students in ways that teachers themselves can see'.[136]

Ethos-School Culture and the Centrality of the Child

A deep sense of the value of people both as participants and as beneficiaries and *ethos-school culture* dovetail and are interdependent aspects of life in the school. However, ethos-school culture warrants special mention. In the foregoing section we looked at people – adults who bring the organisation to life.[137] It is a fact that the role of the school is to identify, satisfy and protect the physical, mental, moral, social, cultural and religious development of pupils. In *Putting Children First*, V. Washington, an American educator, states that in creating an ideal world for children, caring relationships are the soul of productive human existence. It is through these relationships 'that most individuals thrive, learn, and grow'.[138] The quality of care of teachers, institutions and the local community is essential to the proper growth and development of the child.[139]

In the context of schools and schooling children are central to education, and schooling is part of the education process. Indeed, schools and structures are in place because of children, while other members of the wider community are increasingly becoming a part of the school. The purpose of education is to enable young people to manage themselves and their lives effectively and to make the world a better and happier place and in so doing move towards 'new possibilities of fuller and richer life individually and collectively'.[140] If we are proponents of 'whole child' development, then the physical, mental, moral, social, cultural and religious development of the child-pupil will be of paramount importance.[141] In the context of schools and schooling it is important to remember that children 'are part of the culture in which they grow up. They are also deeply connected with the people they live with and meet'.[142] Life within the school, as well as work methods, should feed into and reflect the experience of the child 'him/herself and the family and socio-cultural setting'.[143] This does not always happen, particularly in the case of socio-economically disadvantaged pupils. What often arises in these settings is what the literature refers to as a discontinuity between the home life and the school life of the child.[144] P. Whitaker, head teacher and lecturer in Nottingham, advises teachers 'to be careful to create opportunities for variety to be celebrated and learned about'.[145]

Writing some years later, Whitaker says that 'culture refers to the ways in which … staff and pupils – experience their day-to-day work, and the extent to which they feel able to commit themselves to the tasks and activities they are responsible for'.[146] For L. Stoll and D. Fink, both international experts in educational management and school effectiveness, the definition is somewhat similar 'culture describes how things are and acts as a screen or lens through which the world is viewed'.[147] Whitaker speaks of 'cultural zones' characterised by comfort, danger, uncertainty, confusion, control, achievement, failure, blame and 'the inner turmoils they have generated'.[148] Under the term 'cultural transactions' Whitaker compares the business world – 'relating to the hardware and software of information technology systems' – with the more 'people-focused organizations like primary schools'.[149] 'Cultural forces' refer to 'the powerful inner forces at work' in schools, which are 'neither tangible nor visible', but exercise 'a relentless … power over us'.[150] For Whitaker these cultural forces can be 'the history and traditions' or a 'set of unwritten taboos to be observed'.[151]

Culture is very powerful, 'much too strong to be influenced for any length of time (or at all in some cases) by single, passing projects – no matter how well designed'.[152] Differing somewhat in view are Stoll and Fink who believe that culture is created by 'participants' and 'it inevitably changes as participants change, although it can be a stabilising force'.[153] They conclude that the appointment of a new principal or a development plan 'can change a school's culture'.[154]

When the organisation or the school is 'considered as a whole', where participants are viewed as an 'organizational community', Whitaker refers to this composition as the 'cultural dimensions'. Included in this bracket are stability-instability; integration-separation; and an innovative-resistant approach.[155] Part of the role of management is concerned with 'balancing these awkward and often unpredictable movements, and the effects they have on the individuals concerned'.[156]

D. Hopkins and his colleagues, all in the University of Cambridge, believe that for a proper understanding of culture we must differentiate between 'structure' and 'culture', while both are 'interdependent'.[157] They hold that it is easier to change structures than cultures. They warn of the danger of radical structure change without proper attention to the culture where one 'may get the appearance of change...but not the reality of change'.[158]

Hargreaves, speaking on 'restructuring', puts the distinction this way:

> It is not possible to establish productive school cultures without prior changes being effected in school structure that increase the opportunities for meaningful working relationships and collegial support between teachers.[159]

These authors synchronise on the notion of structures and culture. School culture is 'inextricably linked to structure'.[160]

Whitaker, in his comprehensive analysis of culture, speaks of 'cultural toxins' and 'cultural nutrients'. For him, cultural toxins are 'verbal and non-verbal behaviours, which activate particular emotions such as fear, anger, resentment and jealousy'.[161] The toxins result in 'painful and inhibiting feelings'.[162] On the other hand cultural nutrients 'arouse positive and pleasurable emotions, such as excitement, joy, delight, happiness and affection' in people.[163] The resultant behaviour is an experience of 'being valued, being encouraged, being noticed, being trusted, being listened to, being respected'.[164] When cultural nutrients abound there will be truly cooperative classrooms where 'the adults are themselves learners, very aware of the varieties of ways in which they learn and are therefore always looking for new ways to enable individual children to learn ... It is, above all else, an organisation centred on children and adults as learners'.[165]

We need to know background information of the school and how it functions. We need to know its history, philosophy, management structure, policies, out-of-school activities, its attitudes towards Religious Education, curriculum, parents, pupils and much more. We can learn through asking questions, listening, observing and probing. However, the ethos – school culture 'that indefinable "feel" which defines the sort of community that the school is, how the staff treat the pupils, how the pupils treat one another, and which differentiates one school from another – cannot be learnt from studying the school prospectus'.[166]

Organisations, groups, schools faced with similar environments and circumstances respond differently. The path the school pursues will not result solely from an action plan either, but will come 'under influence from the attitudes, values and perceptions which are common among the members'.[167] Management, too, plays its role, interacting with people and building on the experience of each. So management contributes to the current and evolving culture of schools. 'It is important therefore to recognise the significance of the cultural aspects of management'.[168]

The Convention on the Rights of the Child recognised that we should provide direction to the child's right to freedom of thought 'in a manner consistent with the evolving capacities of the child,' and to the child's freedom of expression 'in accordance with the age and maturity of the child'.[169] The development of identity, self-image, social cooperation, communication, peer relationships, child-to-child learning, child-adult interactions, equality between boy/girl roles (while at the same time recognising and valuing individual differences and special needs) is vital. R.A. Hart, the director of a research group on children's environments, holds that 'the best opportunities for democratic experiences for children come from sustained involvement in a group'.[170] His goal was 'not to encourage the development of "children's power" or to see children operate as an entirely independent sector of their community'[171], but rather to foster 'models of genuine participation' between children, teenagers and adults'.[172] Since post-primary schools are more inaccessible to parents than primary schools there is need to develop other channels to ascertain parent and pupil perspectives. This can be achieved through primary school visits when teacher and pupil perspectives can be highlighted.[173]

In addition to the background in Chapter Two, we note here that four possible roles for parents have been identified.[174] The roles are the parent as supporter/learner, the parent as consumer, the parent as independent, and the parent as participant.[175] C. Vincent, a researcher in the University of Warwick, suggests:

that a sizeable proportion of parents reject the first two models and adopt the third, parent as independent … these parents have minimal contact with the school. The fourth model, parent as participant, is the least common, and also the only option to offer opportunities for the exercise of individual and collective voice.[176]

As outlined in Chapters Two and Three, the role of the parent as prime educator is of paramount importance, but 'the degree to which this applies in individual cases and the kinds of support systems needed to enable the role to be discharged optimally' requires much attention.[177] The family, however constituted, 'is seen as the child's most important setting' for survival and for healthy 'physical, affective and cognitive development'.[178]

CHAPTER SIX

Conclusions and Challenges

SINCE THE RESEARCH[1] for this book dealt with a recent development in Irish education, one which is on-going, a definitive judgement such as one might make about an educational phenomenon in another century is not possible. Nonetheless, the HSCL Scheme, which was the broad topic of this book, received some serious evaluation in the work of the author. It is now appropriate to indicate some of the strands that come together as this book draws to a close.

The Views of Educators

Throughout the book the views of educators were noted regarding new visions in education which called for partnership especially between home and school and also community. Something that is more subtle – authors grasping at less tangible but decisive issues like attitudes, prejudice and the need to break out of set patterns – was also noted. Leading educators, therefore, not only showed some consensus on need, but also an emerging consensus on the necessity of developing partnership through practical measures and through a re-education and re-orientation in attitudes.

The Need

Socio-economic and educational disadvantage, including 'uninvolved' parents, have become issues in educational circles across the developed and developing world since the early 1960s. The theme of disadvantage is central to every chapter in this book. It is central for two reasons. Firstly, as has just been noted, it is an issue emerging, studied and responded to worldwide. Most specifically, the HSCL Scheme emerged from the Department of Education precisely in answer to deprivation and need.

Socio-economic Disadvantage and the Marginalised Pupil

It was observed in Chapter One that the term disadvantage is an ambiguous one. It was recognised how and why policymakers, educators and social scientists grapple with the concept. However, the focus of all groups would be to ease the effects of disadvantage on individuals and groups and, if possible, to break the cycle of disadvantage, particularly for children. The alteration of school structures and practices, a more enlightened and positive way of viewing both marginalised pupils and their families and effective schooling are called for. In considering the views of educators the debate regarding language 'deficit' and 'difference' has been postulated. In addition the argument relating to 'continuity' and 'discontinuity' between the home and school experiences of marginalised children was examined. The influential role of the home and the community is central to the entire book.

A pupil is socially bonded to the extent that he/she is attached to adults and peers, committed to the ethos of the school and involved in school activities with a belief in the legitimacy of schooling. Obviously the more parents know about the school, the more they can socialise their children to schooling. The committed pupil remains in school to graduation spurred on by internalised goals emanating from the home, the school and wider society.

Uninvolved Parents

Despite educational theory emphasising the role of parents, educational practice has lingered behind. The formation and culture of teachers did not lead to their having a strong practical conviction about the role of parents in the school, parents as prime educators. It was taken for granted that the axiom 'parents as prime educators' referred to what went on at home. From a teacher's point, therefore, there was an absence of a positive appreciation of the possible role of parents. There was a negative apprehension in which parents were seen as threatening, intrusive, a nuisance, not really understanding the school and not professional.[2] It is important when seeking to change school culture to see the teacher as the medium through which the change must pass, otherwise the change may be resisted or shaped in an unintended way.[3] From the point of view of parents, especially in marginalised areas, but also among the socio-economic lower middle-class parents, there is a consciousness of the teacher as being better educated and, to that extent at least, the expert.[4] Again, parents of the marginalised, working and lower middle-class frequently have unhealed memories of their own unhappy school days, which were often, but not always, associated with their self-image and lack of achievement. Furthermore parents were not encouraged to take an active interest in what went on in the school. They were seen as supportive of the school in matters of discipline, homework and fundraising. From the 1960s onwards people became aware of the gap between educational theory on the role of parents and the actual practice. Two things happened. Firstly, educationalists began to notice that there was a gap. Secondly, this gap gave rise to more theories and – more significantly – to specific action in various places.

An example of such action is the HSCL Scheme, the subject of this book

An 'Answer' to the Need

It is now appropriate to turn to the specifics of the HSCL Scheme, which are highlighted in this book, as the services to disadvantaged areas both in a general way and in the specific sense of the HSCL Scheme are considered.

General Services to Schools Serving Disadvantaged Pupils

Initiatives have been in place for decades to help disadvantaged pupils at primary and post-primary levels. These services are outlined in Chapters One and Three. Suffice to say that these services, supports and schemes range from the school meals service, free-book/book-rental scheme, through to an increased *per capita* grant to principals and chairpersons. Concessionary posts have been allocated to most schools in designated areas of disadvantage and curriculum adaptation to meet the needs of the less academic pupil has been a commitment of the Irish Government in the White Paper on Educational Development (1980).

The HSCL Scheme as an 'Answer' in Relation to Parent Empowerment

Firstly, the HSCL Scheme is an answer in so far as parental development and involvement is taking place. The value of the home and its influence on the life of the young person is clearly outlined in this book. The HSCL Scheme is a targeted and focused resource, aimed at the most marginalised within the designated schools. This is positive discrimination in favour of the most marginalised.

The HSCL Scheme as an 'Answer' Regarding Teacher and 'Whole School' Development

Teachers were more likely than principals or coordinators to have the perception that there is little or no consultation with parents.[5] This finding could portray a lack of communication at staff level, a withholding of information, an unclear view of the situation as it is, or a desire for the system that could be or should be on the part of principals in particular. It was noted that 54 per cent of teachers had 'no understanding' of partnership and the fact that teachers were the least positive about partnership was also observed.[6] There is a need for teacher development in order to promote in-school, inter-school and intra-school change and development. 'The rules of the world are changing. It is time for the rules of teaching and teachers' work to change with them'.[7]

The urgent need within the HSCL Scheme is for systematic and regular teacher development to allow each teacher to become a 'home-school teacher' in attitude. It is especially important to note that 'parent involvement practices succeed with less-educated parents and disadvantaged students, where it is crucial that the school make a difference'.[8] School is the centre of change and exists within the context of home, community, voluntary and statutory agencies, religious bodies and affiliations, educational organisations and institutions and the Government. Each group has an agenda, has self-interest to protect. Schools can, as many do, 'isolate themselves to maintain control and avoid criticism. In so doing, they not only build barriers against potential partners; they contribute to the incoherence of pupils' lives'.[9] In the next section we shall examine this intricate network and the role of the HSCL local coordinator within it.

The Local HSCL Coordinator

Given the analysis summarised above, which itself is amply documented in contemporary educational literature, it is clear that there are two foci in the learning ellipse – namely, school and the home, each needing the other. In the HSCL Scheme which emerged from the Department of Education a third component was identified, namely, the community. It might be argued that in the future it is the development of the community dimension that will lead to the greatest challenge and fruits. The home and the school interaction are relatively well advanced where the HSCL Scheme has been initiated.

However, even going back to the first two, home and school, we had two moral bodies separated by a chasm over which there was no obvious or reliable bridge. This book postulates that the coordinator is an important link agent in the partnership enterprise of the HSCL Scheme. Chapters Three and Four focus on the role of the coordinator as the key link agent between three existing bodies – home, school and community. The contribution of the Irish scheme compared with those examined in other countries was the clear identification of the need of a bridge, which would be the coordinator. Then it was clear that the coordinator needed a status and the freedom from actual teaching commitments to fulfil this bridge role. It is this centring of the role of the coordinator that makes the Irish scheme unique and one could argue an important development in educational theory and practice. The question of community brings in many more complex issues to the above role of the coordinator. It is relatively easy to establish parameters for the activity of the coordinator, for example welcoming parents to the school, home visitation and parent development. It is also relatively easy to identify the skills needed for coordinators and to provide training and support systems.

However, to use traditional terminology, found especially in Catholic social writings but with roots in Greek political thinking, both the school and the family are 'imperfect societies', which means that they do not have within themselves all the resources needed to fulfil their aim, in this case, the education of the child. As 'imperfect societies' they need the community. We have already referred to the complexity of the notion of community and the pluriform usage of the word. Hence, though most people would readily admit to a role for the community in education, the specification of this role and its actualisation is a difficult task, and one which varies from place to place.

The questionnaires were interesting for the rather low estimation in theory and in practice of the community in the educational task.[10] Here again there is need of a mediator bringing together the community and the school, the community and the family. This mediator is of course the coordinator. There is a discernible change regarding community in recent times in the HSCL Scheme brought about through the understanding of the coordinator, the understanding that the marginalised family/families need to access those meaning systems that complement and do not replace their own meaning systems. The Local Committee, which deals with issues in the community that impinge on learning is an example of proactive change, when functioning well.

Strengths in the Role of the Coordinator

As has already been stated, the HSCL Scheme is centred on the adults within the school community whose attitudes and behaviour impinge on the life of the pupil.

Bearing in mind that the role of the coordinator is targeted and focused on the most marginalised families within the school community, it follows that these families would have young people who are potential and even likely drop-outs from the school system.[11] We first look at the strengths in the role of the coordinator in relation to the young person in danger of dropping out of school. We have already named the value of prevention, that is, precluding the occurrence of problems and if not, then 'intervention during the early development of difficulties' as a key feature of liaison.[12] Schools alone cannot solve the multifaceted problems of 'at risk' families – 'responsibility must be shared and collectively assumed, rather than the cosy option of apportioning blame and then walking away'.[13] Hence, the coordinator initiates support services that are home-family based, school based and community based.

Home-based initiatives include the coordinator visiting parents at home, training and providing parent-to-parent home visitation, providing for homework support within the home or local community and supporting teenage parents to stay on at school through the intervention of third level students as mentors. Where these initiatives have taken place there is a level of satisfaction, particularly on the part of parents.[14] All of the foregoing initiatives are backed up by research evidence world-wide and now by practice here in Ireland. This aspect of the HSCL Scheme should be further developed and promoted as a way of enabling the home to acknowledge, work on and eventually solve many of its own needs and problems. Parents within the HSCL Scheme often call for support and skills in managing their children's behaviour in the home. This request, together with the identification of similar needs by the school, has led coordinators to provide a school-based support service.

Among the school-based services provided by the coordinator for parents are the parents' room and crèche facilities, courses, classes and activities, involvement in policy formation and opportunities for parents to act as a resource to the school and the school community, and the coordinators' availability to the parents. It seems clear from the research findings[15] and through interaction on the field that the coordinator has functioned well with parents in the above named areas.

On the other hand, school-based supports for teachers are not so much in evidence, with calls from principals and from coordinators themselves throughout the findings[16] for renewed efforts to involve teachers. There is a danger that 'each side of the school-family partnership can relieve its disappointment and sense of failure by judging the other to have been deficient in the task'.[17] However, one must remember that the primary task of teachers is to provide a rich learning environment for pupils and it may be more realistic to expect that the time already given to parents need not be increased, but should, in the words of a renowned educator, be a 'respectful intervention'.[18] For this to happen we would require a pooling of resources of home and school in order that the pupil may enjoy childhood and that academic progress may be in harmony with ability. Educational partnership can be viewed as 'the proper relationship between one child's parent(s) and that child's teachers(s) about that individual child's education acquired both at home and at school'.[19] It can be said that the coordinator is the bridge between parents and teachers that has allowed this to happen.

Pupils are not only members of families and schools, they are also part of community groups, churches, teams, clubs and gangs. An integrated approach means recognising all the influences at work, aiming to bring coherence to the multiple messages young people receive.[20] Acceptance of the value of the community dimension of the HSCL Scheme has been growing from the mid-1990s. This growth has accelerated since then with the development of Local Committees and the general emphasis on the community in current literature.

A particular strength of the coordinator, in relation to the community dimension of HSCL, is the ability to network with agencies and to direct parents towards existing services either within or outside their local community. A further strength in the role of the coordinator is his/her willingness to delegate to local community personnel as is evidenced by parents and teachers working together in small groups. This now calls for the inclusion of community agencies. In addition the recruiting of parents, the training of parents as facilitators and leadership training all enhance the community dimension. The training of parents as home visitors, the facilitation of Local Committee meetings and the giving of parent-to-parent input at meetings all denote a sophisticated level of community involvement in education. Parent responsibility for the maintenance of the parents' room and the running of the crèche present a human way of school-community integration. By way of conclusion it can be said that the coordinator has facilitated the growth of the school towards being a part of the community. The coordinator has contributed to the fact that the community is supporting the school and working in its interests. In short the role of the coordinator has been to intervene respectfully and to encourage this growth towards autonomy and interdependence.

In this section we have named some of the strengths of the coordinator in supporting the whole family, rather than the young person in isolation. Next, we considered the role of the coordinator in providing support services within schools. Finally, we viewed the interconnection of school and community and how the community can grow through processes generated from within and by the community. The role of the coordinator is a vital bridge linking any two of these interconnections and also linking all three.

Weaknesses in the Role of the Coordinator
The weaknesses in the work of the coordinator were discovered following the coding of questionnaire responses throughout 1997.[21] This data bank supported my personal knowledge of the scheme gleaned from visiting schools and training coordinators. The areas that emerged as requiring

attention were home visiting by the coordinator, the training of parents as home visitors, policy formation – including parental and community involvement – and planning, monitoring and evaluating as part of the role of the coordinator. There is also need for a continuing focus on the integrated delivery of service to marginalised children and their families, the delegation process, the delivery of in-career development by the coordinators to staff and to themselves and the development of Local Committees.

Two of the above named areas, that of policy formation and the delivery of in-career development by the coordinators, were facilitated through the practice of action research, carried out 'always and explicitly, to improve practice'.[22] The other shortcomings were dealt with through the support structures of the scheme and particularly through in-career development. It can be stated, therefore, that this book is the product of both formative and summative evaluation.

An area of concern, and one that emerged as a surprise, was the almost irrelevance of home visitation throughout the research findings.[23] This is indeed a weakness on the part of the coordinator and one that has been addressed many times at in-career development since this data was coded. It is the view of the Department of Education that coordinators need to be continually encouraged to spend the required 30 to 40 per cent of their time on home visitation. The physical and emotional drain on the coordinator can be very challenging and may often go unnoticed or unappreciated by school personnel. However, coordinators always speak of the power of home visits in bonding with the family and, ultimately, in improving educational opportunity for young people. This view point was indeed supported by parents.

The training of parents as home visitors has taken almost five years to establish in some areas and is currently working well. Some coordinators are not yet convinced of its value despite wide experience on the part of the Bernard van Leer Foundation across the world and that of other coordinators here in Ireland. As was indicated in the research findings[24] there was an absence of planning, monitoring and evaluating across the research population. This was also the case in relation to coordinators although the lack was not so acute. While planning and evaluating were priority areas for coordinators from the inception of the HSCL Scheme, there has been a direct focus on this work from the mid-1990s to date. Coordinators were led through theory and practical processes until a satisfactory schema was established. The work to establish Local Committees across new schools in the scheme is now in train. Coordinators have adopted a team approach in their introduction and development with the inclusion of pupils.

From the foregoing the formative nature of the evaluation can be gleaned. The summative element is obvious.

Towards the Future

At this stage, it can be argued that an initiative has been taken in Irish education that, in many ways, amounts to a serious culture change for teachers in particular, namely a new way of relating between school and home. It is likewise a culture shock for parents. It is gratifying to be able to note the visionary analysis by the often maligned Department of Education in the continual inter-departmental infighting for funds, which is a mark of all democratic governments. The Department of Education managed not only to acquire funds, but also to allocate them seriously to this new scheme. It is also worth noting that enthusiasm and goodwill are found not only in the Department of Education, but throughout the areas in which the scheme has been operating. It is, therefore, all the more urgent to look to some present weaknesses and some undeveloped areas so that the scheme may become more sharply focused.

Home visitation is carried out by the coordinator. This is one of the major challenges in reaching families who are most in need of support and is emphasised for the purpose of 'forming bonds of trust'. Through home visitation, self-reliance rather than increased dependence can be fostered and family self-image can be enhanced rather than stigmatised for its inadequacies. It is vital for the life of the scheme, not to mention its on-going development, that coordinators remain sharply focused on this aspect of their work.

The involvement of parents as home visitors 'transfers them ... from being passive and dependent recipients of assistance ... to becoming active members of the community able to give to others, and consequently, able to take pride in themselves'.[25] This type of intervention-service enables individuals and the community at large to respond more effectively to the problems and challenges facing it. Coordinators require further training and skills development in this area of their work in order that they can proceed with conviction and determination. Principals need to be more open to this process of growth within their school and the wider school community. Parents require further training in their role as change agents within the home-community.

Policy formation – parents and teachers working together on policy formation was a highly successful practice in 94 per cent of the HSCL schools in 1997-1998. It is important that this process of bringing parents and teachers together be continued and extended to include community members. Support from the Board of Management and from principals is required, so that the coordinators can view the inclusion of marginalised but developed parents in policy formation as an on-going feature of their work and may have the freedom to organise it.

Planning, monitoring and evaluating are part of the role of the coordinator. It is required of them that they carry out these functions at 'family cluster' and 'local cluster' levels[26] and that they work as teams across the designated schools in their areas. It is also anticipated that the skills coordinators have learned during in-career development sessions and through their practice will be transferred at staff level.

The delegation process within the parameters of the HSCL Scheme continues to be an area which requires monitoring. It is normal when one is successful at a given task, particularly a task with a community dimension, to want to maintain the lead role. The aim of the HSCL Scheme is to allow the 'para-professional' be the front-line worker while the coordinator takes an ancillary role. It is incumbent on coordinators to keep the delegation focus clearly in mind from the very early stages of programme development so that the local community may take over the work and carry it on.

The delivery of in-career development by the coordinators is a practice in delegation that is functioning well at both staff level and during their own in-career development sessions. This practice should continue to be enhanced, particularly in relation to teacher development and growth.

Teacher development is the hinge on which the foregoing recommendations revolve. To a degree, coordinators can redress most of the above challenges over time. However, quality renewal within schools will be determined by attitudinal change on the part of principals and teachers, brought about through team development.

In designated areas of disadvantage team development must include training for teachers in an understanding of poverty and marginalisation. The location of poverty, how it impacts on the lives of children, families and communities and an understanding of the environment and context in which children live and learn is essential. The raising of poverty issues within schools and supporting the development of appropriate preventative methodologies, strategies and practices is of paramount importance. The purpose and process of *poverty proofing* which 'assesses policies and programmes at design and review stages in relation to the likely impact that they will have or have had on poverty and inequalities' is incumbent on all schools.[27]

In order that schools may have the vision and courage to face the above demands, a very different type of in-career development is required for the staff. In-career development that focuses on the person of the teacher, and acknowledges the tremendous contribution teachers make to society now and will make in the future, is urgently needed. It can be difficult for teachers to render a service, to remain positive, hopeful and committed when faced, at times, with unreasonable demands and negative publicity.

The development of *Local Committees* was slow, particularly in the early years of the scheme. The Local Committee can be viewed as a mechanism of community self-help and self-functioning through defining community needs, establishing priorities and developing local resources, particularly people resources. It can be said that Local Committees have focused their attention on the link between poverty in the community, school failure and the continuing cycle of disadvantage. Local Committees aim at the preventing families from becoming 'at risk' rather than at compensation for its damaging effects. It can be said, from experience in schools and from research, that the Local Committee promotes and contributes to the *integrated delivery of service* to marginalised children and their families. Since the 'at risk' factor extends beyond the child, 'when a society has a great number of children and families at risk, the society itself is at risk',[28] it is almost binding on the school community to facilitate the coordinators in having a dynamic 'community committee' in the Local Committee.

However, much growth has taken place within schools in the foregoing areas. Included are teacher involvement with parents, particularly in the areas of collaborative policy making, home visits by coordinators, parents as home visitors, Local Committees, transfer programmes, further development with regard to parents in the classroom and a more inclusive type of parent-teacher meeting. Some coordinators have included primary or post-primary pupils on the Local Committee and in policy formation with parents, teachers and community members. This development is affirmed and its extension is further encouraged. HSCL coordinators need to be acknowledged for their openness, ability and the level they have reached in providing an *integrated delivery of service* to marginalised children and their families-communities. They are, no doubt the forerunners in this field.

The HSCL Scheme 'is now the cornerstone and force for integration of service in all Department strategies that are designed to address educational disadvantage and early school leaving'.[29] From its inception, in 1990, the HSCL Scheme has led the way in networking and integration. With the advent of Early Start, Breaking the Cycle – urban and rural, the Support Teacher Project, the 8-15 Early School Leaver Initiative (ESLI)[30] and the Stay in School Retention Initiative (SSRI) the integration of services to marginalised children and their families-communities became a crucial item on the agenda for National Coordinators. The quality effectiveness of *an integrated delivery of service* in all schemes/supports to marginalised children and their families-communities calls for *serious evaluation* on a number of levels. Firstly, there is need for evaluation on the quality of interrelation between all

Department of Education schemes. Secondly, evaluation on the degree to which their interrelatedness contributes, broadly speaking, to the desired educational outcome for the marginalised is essential. Thirdly, the way in which the Department of Education schemes integrate with those from the different Departments of the Government and the other statutory, voluntary and Church providers requires evaluation. The integrated delivery of service in marginalised communities is vital. This calls for a partnership approach from all those who are 'building people to put talent to work'.[31]

In conclusion, the evidence acquired for the research and its analysis[32] point to the fact that the role of the local HSCL coordinator has not only been crucial for the scheme up to now, but will also be critical in addressing these weaknesses. One last point is the need for coordinators to be affirmed by principals, teachers, management, parents and by each other so that they will be encouraged and, as appropriate, directed in the future evolution of the HSCL Scheme.

Notes

Chapter One: Marginalisation

1   See Johnston and Borman, 1992:3-28.

2   Archer, 2001:200.

3   Kellaghan, Weir, Ó Huallacháin and Morgan, 1995:2.

4   Ibid.

5   Kellaghan, Weir, Ó hUallacháin and Morgan, 1995:30.

6   See Conaty, 1999 and 2000.

7   Schorr,1988a: xxiii, see also Bacik and O'Connell 1998.

8   Pallas, Natriello and McDill, 1989:17.

9   Ibid. See also Cullen, 1997:5 and OECD, 1995:20-24, 48.

10 Kellaghan, Weir, Ó hUallacháin and Morgan, 1995:2.

11 European White Paper, 1995:10, see also 62-66.

12 NAPS, 1997:9, see also NESF 1997a and 1997b.

13 Inter-Departmental Policy Committee 1999, and Ireland's National Report on the Implementation of the Outcome of the UN World Summit for Social Development 2000.

14 Johnston and O'Brien, 2000:55.

15 The Bernard van Leer Foundation is based in Holland but has world wide practice in early childhood and community development within marginalised areas.

16 Johnston, 1992:111, cited in Johnston and Borman.

17 Lynch, 1989:33.

18 Clark, 1992:75, cited in Johnston and Borman.

19 Hargreaves, Earl and Ryan, 1997:159.

20   Ibid.

21   European White Paper, 1995:57.

22   NEPS, 1997:39.

23   Tinto, 1993:140, see also Moxley et al, 2001.

24   Ibid., 212.

25   Wehlage, Rutter, Smith, Lesko and Fernandez, 1989:113-133; see also Cusick and Wheeler, 1988:273-276.

26   Ibid., 118.

27   Ibid.

28   See Ryan, 2001.

29   Corson, 1998:85.

30   NESF, Report No. 11, 1997a and Report No. 12, 1997b.

31   Welling, 1985 at Community Education Development Centre in Coventry.

Chapter Two: Attempts to Deal with Marginalisation

1   Wolfendale, 1983:155.

2   Article 42.

3   The European Convention on Human Rights Strasbourg, 1984:28.

4   Maastricht Treaty, 1992:126 (12).

5   Macbeth and Ravn, 1994:12.

6   Coolahan, 1994:23.

7   Department of Education, Primary Education Review Body (PERB), 1990:36.

8   Conaty 1999.

9   Department of Education, 1992:140-141.

10   NPC-P, 1993:7-8.

11   Conaty 1999.

12   NPC-P, 1993:Foreward.

13   Department of Education, 1995:140.

14   Ibid.

15   Department of Education, circular 24/91 National Schools, and circular M27/91 Post-Primary Schools.

16   Department of Education 1995:141.

17   Irish Government, 1998: Article 26.

18   Department of Education, 1994:13

19   OECD, 1991:31, Department of Education, 1995:142, see also Education Act, 1998, Department of Education 2000:3 (Cromien Report)
20   Wolfendale, 1983: 14.
21   See Drudy and Lynch, 1993 and Kellaghan et al. 1993.
22   Barker, 1987:5.
23   Bernstein cited in Tizard and Hughes, 1984.
24   Tizard and Hughes, 1984:143.
25   Widlake, 1986:12.
26   Drudy and Lynch, 1993:151.
27   Tizard and Hughes, 1984:160.
28   Ibid., 16.
29   Ibid., 16-17.
30   Ibid., 249.
31   Ibid.
32   Ibid.
33   Ibid., 251-252).
34   Bronfenbrenner, 1974:27.
35   Tizard and Hughes, 1984:252.
36   Kellaghan et al., 1993:41.
37   Tizard, Schofield and Hewison, 1982:14.
38   de Jong, 1993:201-213.
39   Ibid., 51.
40   Cited in Goode, 1987:112.
41   Ibid., 118.
42   Macbeth, 1989:69.
43   Macbeth, 1984: 184.
44   Freire, and Shor, 1987:29-30.
45   See also South and Crowder, 1977.
46   Widlake, 1986:16.
47   Halton, Munns and Dent, 1996:42, see also O'Sullivan, 1980:138-142.
48   Drudy and Lynch, 1993:154.
49   Ibid.
50   Ibid.
51   Pallas, Natriello and Mc Dill, 1989:16.
52   Ibid.
53   Comer, 1988a:24-25.
54   Ibid.

55 Comer, 1986:446.
56 Voiced by The Open University in 1977:12.
57 McAllister Swap, 1990a:9.
58 Clark, 1992.
59 Youngman, 1978.
60 CMRS, 1992:8-9.
61 Kellaghan et al., 1993:27, see also Evans, 1998.
62 Taylor, 1980:17.
63 Seeley, 1981:65.
64 Cited in Dulles, 1987:47.
65 Ibid.
66 See discussion in Dulles, 1987:47-50.
67 Midwinter, 1980:206.
68 Bronfenbrenner, 1974:49 and Galloway, Rogers, Armstrong and Leo, 1998.
69 Roland-Martin, 1995:359.
70 BvLF, 1984:22.
71 Elder, 1990:50-54.
72 See also Rutherford and Billig, 1995:64-68.
73 MacBeath, 1999:14.
74 Welling, 1988:13.
75 McLaughlin and Irby, 1994:301.
76 Ibid., see also Donthwaite, 1992.
77 Paz, 1990:19.
78 Ibid., 3.
79 Schorr, 1988:257.
80 Welling, 1988:12-13, see also Macleod 1989.
81 Catterall, 1998:302 and Barber, 1993.
82 Paz, 1990:7 and Nimnicht, Arango and Hearn, 1987.
83 Widlake, 1986:47.
84 Freire, 1972:25, see also Cropley, 1981:57-69.
85 Watt, 1989:196, see also Blasé, 1994 and Mortimore et al., 1995.
86 MacBeath, 1996:144, see also Craig, 1995a and 1995b.
87 Paulo Freire, 1982.
88 Macbeth, 1989:3.
89 Department of Education, 1971:12-17.
90 See Halliday, 1996.
91 McAllister Swap, 1990a:11.
92 Elliot-Kemp and Elliot-Kemp, 1992:66.

93   Roberts, 1980:50.

94   Ibid., see also Gray and Wilcox, 1995; Halliday, 1996; Brookfield, 1995; Cullingford, 1995; Dalin et al., 1993; Schön, 1987 and Zeichner, 1996.

95   Resnik, 1987:18, see also Yánez, 1998.

96   See Mc Carthy and Gardner, 1993.

97   Widlake, 1986:119.

98   Ericson and Elleth, 1990:9, see also Smit and van Esch, 1994.

99   Lumby, 1999:71-83, see also Preedy, Glatter and Levacic, 1997 and Short et al., 1994.

100   See Epstein, 1987:6-9; Davies, 1991:376-382; Dowling and Osborne, 1994 and Salole, 1992.

101   Freire and Shor, 1987:24, see also Pedersen, Faucher and Eaton, 1978:29 and Short, 1985.

102   Delgado-Gaitan, 1991:37, see also Topping and Wolfendale, 1985 and Scaparro, 19944.

103   See Avalos, 1992:433; Seashore et al., 1995 and Robertson, 1995.

104   Midwinter, 1980:204, see also Philip and Chetley, 1988.

105   Comer, 1980:69.

106   Fullan and Stiegelbauer, 1991:81, see also Caldwell and Spinks, 1988.

107   Wehlage et al., 1989:149-150 and Delgado-Gaitan et al., 1991.

108   Ibid.

109   Wehlage et al., 1989:12, see also Troyer and Younts, 1997.

110   McAllisterSwap, 1990b:33, see also Short 1985.

111   Testerman, 1996:364, see also Atkinson 1994a and 1994b.

112   Widlake, 1986:121.

113   Beattie, 1995:66, see also Covey 1992 and Alrichter et al., 1993.

114   Nisbet and Watt, 1984:63.

115   Widlake, 1986:121, see also Woodward and Beckman-Woodward, 1994, and Mezirow, 1990 and 1991.

116   Cross, 1990:22, see also Lomax, 1996.

117   Wolfendale, 1983:15.

118   Freire, 1972:43.

119   Wolfendale, 1983:14.

120   Delgado-Gaitan, and Allexsacht-Snider, 1992:79-80.

121   Cited in Delgado-Gaitan, and Allexsacht-Snider, 1992:81.

122   Roberts, 1980:48.

123   Ibid., 52.

124   Lynch, 1989:134.
125   Midwinter, 1980:204.
126   Cattermole and Robinson, 1985:48 see also Krumm, 1994 and Harris et al., 1996.
127   Seeley, 1981:11.
128   Ibid., 76, Bogdanowicz, 1994 and Bastiani, 1987.
129   Brantlinger and Majd-Jabbari, 1998:442-443.
130   Block, 1993:32.
131   Atkin et al., 1988:14.
132   Ibid., 15.
133   Wolfendale, 1983:69.
134   See Salole, 1992.
135   See Widlake, 1986 and Widlake and Macleod, 1984.
136   Widlake, 1986:62.
137   Atkin, Bastiani and Goode, 1988.
138   Bastiani, 1989:9.
139   See Whalley, 1994.
140   Early Start Pre-school project located in 40 areas of educational disadvantage in Ireland
141   Edwards and Redfern, 1988.
142   Comer, 1980, 1988a, 1988b, Sallis, 1988, Mufson, Cooper and Hall, 1989 and Elder, 1990.
143   See Krasnow, 1990a and 1990b also Rosenholtz, 1985:352-388.
144   See Mc Allister Swap 1990a and 1990b also Wilton, 1975.
145   BvLF, 1988.
146   Paz, 1990:19.
147   BvLF, 1986:6.
148   Bendure and Friary, 1984:505-507.
149   Cohen, 1991:2.
150   Pantin, 1979:11.
151   Cohen, 1991:4.
152   Bourne, 1983:146.
153   Pantin, 1979:74-75.
154   Ibid., 76.
155   Cohen, 1991:3.
156   Bourne, 1983:144-145.
157   Cohen, 1991: 23.
158   Ibid., 55.
159   Pantin, 1984:38.

160   Ibid.
161   Cohen, 1991:5.
162   Ibid., 61.
163   Paz, 1990:31
164   Ibid.
165   Ibid., 32.
166   Ibid., 53.
167   Ibid., 38.
168   Ibid.
169   Ibid., 39.
170   Ibid.
171   Salach, 1993:94.
172   Ibid., 95.
173   Ibid.
174   Ibid.

Chapter Three: Focus Points: Teacher, Parent, Pupil

1   Rutland St. Pre-school Project, Dublin, Ireland.
2   Ryan, 1994.
3   Conaty, 1999.
4   Circular 24/91 to all National Schools and Circular M27/91 to all
      Post-Primary Schools.
5   Department of Education, 1990.
6   Ibid., 1993.
7   Burkan, 1996:190.
8   Stoll and Fink, 1996:15.
9   Department of Education, 1993.
10   Local Committee – a group of school personnel, voluntary and
      statutory agencies and marginalised but developed parents who
      work on community issues that impinge on learning.
11   Welling, 1985 in the Community Education Development Centre
      (CEDC) in Coventry.
12   Welling, 1988:13.
13   Bernard van Leer Foundation (BvLF) literature (1987-1999), that of
      Pantin, 1979 and 1984, and Mezirow, 1990, 1991, and 1996.
14   Pantin, 1979 and 1984.

15   Bourne, 1983:132.
16   Hatwood-Futrell, 1986:8, see also O'Callaghan, 1993.
17   Paz, 1990.
18   Freire, 1972; Freire and Shor, 1987; Freire 1994 and 1997.
19   Lovett, 1998:148.
20   MacBeath, Mearns and Smith, 1986:264.
21   Government Agency.
22   Area Development Management Ltd. manages the Local Development Social Inclusion Programme that forms part of the National Development Plan.
23   Conaty, 1999:336-342.
24   Ibid., 524.
25   See Fullan, 1995a and 1995b, and Conaty, 1999.
26   National Steering Committee of the HSCL Scheme
27   Department of Education, 1992:6.
28   Ibid., 1990:7.
29   Ibid., 6.
30   Ibid., 1991:6.
31   See Conaty, 1999:108.
32   Ibid.
33   Rae, 1997:13, see also Wills, 1993.
34   Rae, 1997:16.
35   Bramley,1991:xv.
36   Reay, 1994:55.
37   Rae, 1997:75.
38   Bramley, 1991:1-35, see also Hayton, 1999; Galloway et al., 1998 and Smyth, 1999.
39   Conaty, 1999.
40   Ibid.
41   Bramley, 1991:25.
42   Ibid.
43   Department of Education, 1994b.
44   Ibid., 1991:5.
45   The 'Family Cluster' is a group of HSCL coordinators serving the same catchment area. The 'Local Cluster' is a multiple of the 'Family Cluster' and the 'Term Cluster' is a multiple of the 'Local Cluster'. Thirteen 'Regional Cluster Meetings' are held annually. They provide an opportunity for chairpersons, principals, coordinators, inspectors and psychologists, in a particular region, to have

input into the evaluation and development of the HSCL Scheme.

46 Conaty, 1999.

47 Leaving Certificate Applied (an alternative to the traditional Leaving Certificate)

48 See Chen and Stevenson, 1989 and Hill and Cole, 2001.

49 Conaty, 1999.

50 See endnote 22 (this Chapter)

51 Conaty, 1999.

52 Ibid.

53 Department of Education 1, 1992:6.

54 Core group – a group of parents close to the coordinator and his/her work

55 See Sergiovanni, 1994 and 1996 and Sheppard, 1997.

56 Thomson, 1991:195, see also Joyce et al., 1999.

57 Conaty, 1999.

58 Regional Cluster – see endnote 45 – this chapter.

59 See Harris, 2000.

60 See Haynes, 1998.

61 See Strengthening Families for Life, 1998 (Dept. of Social, Community and Family Affairs).

62 OECD, 1998:13.

63 National Children's Strategy, 2000:89.

64 See Partnership 2000 and National Development Plan 2000-2006.

65 Conaty, 1999.

66 Ibid.

67 Ryan, 1994.

68 Ryan, 1996.

69 Conaty, 1999.

70 Kellaghan and Greaney, 1993a.

71 Schweinhart, 1993.

Chapter Four: A Crucial Insight: Partnership

1 Drudy and Lynch, 1993:31-35, see also Lindon, 1998.

2 Ibid., 147-157.

3 Healy, 1992:13.

4 Anglin-Lawlor, 1994.

5   Conaty, 1999 (Chapter 5).
6   Seeley, 1981:65.
7   See Weber, 1947.
8   Bentley, 1996:87-88.
9   Johnson and Redmond, 1998:23.
10   Block, 1993:28.
11   Ibid., xx.
12   Whitehead and Eaton-Whitehead, 1991:27.
13   Block, 1993:32.
14   Ferder and Heagle, 1989:166.
15   Block, 1993:23-32.
16   Ibid., 23.
17   Ibid., 25.
18   Wrigley, 1992.
19   See Hall and Lindzey, 1957 and Jung,1959.
20   Drudy and Uí Chatháin, 1999:3.
21   Ibid.
22   O'Donnell, 1996:173.
23   Ibid.
24   BvLF, 1992:1-24.
25   Ibid., 11.
26   Lareau, 1992:207-208.
27   Ibid., 208.
28   Ibid.
29   Ibid.
30   BvLF, 1992:13.
31   Seeley, 1981:67.
32   Ibid.,102-103.
33   Block, 1993:29.
34   Ibid., 30.
35   Block, 1993:31
36   Iacocca, 1985:56-57.
37   Crowley and Watt, 1992:97.
38   Ruane, 1992:38.
39   Freire, 1972:26.
40   Paz, 1990:17.
41   Block, 1993:41-51.
42   See Endnote 15, Chapter One.
43   Salach, 1993:10-20.

44   BvLF, 1986:14-15.
45   Paz, 1990:2.
46   Salach, 1993:23.
47   Freire, 1972:12.
48   Ibid., 21-22.
49   Ibid., 31.
50   Pignatelli, 1992, see also Short, Greer and Melvin, 1994:38-58.
51   Bastiani, 1988:xvii.
52   Block, 1993:49.
53   Conaty, 1999:359-412.
54   O'Connor, 1993:106
55   Conaty, 1999:315-412.
56   Ibid.
57   Ibid.
58   Ibid.
59   Burkan, 1996:190.
60   Conaty, 1999:315-412.
61   Ibid.

Chapter Five: Practical Steps

1   Hope, Timmel, and Hodzi, 1984:69 Bk 3.
2   Stewart, 1985:93.
3   Hargreaves, 1994:22.
4   Department of Education, 1995:157.
5   Conaty, 1999:232-358, see also Prosser, 1999 and Riley, 1998.
6   Flanagan, Haase, and Walsh, 1995:14, see also Belbin, 1998.
7   Blanchard and O'Connor, 1997:55, see also Civil, 1997.
8   Blanchard, Carew, and Parisi-Carew, 1993:27.
9   Ibid.
10   Pugh and De'Ath, 1989:33, see also Creese, 1995.
11   Clayton, 1997:22.
12   Ibid., 28.
13   The Report on the Commission on Global Governance, 1995:49.
14   Adair, 1988:39.
15   Ibid.
16   Covey and Merrill, 1994:26.
17   Blanchard and O'Connor, 1997:55.

18 Ibid.
19 Ibid.
20 Block, 1993:32.
21 Blanchard and O'Connor, 1997:47-48.
22 Maister, 1997:19.
23 Ibid., 168-169.
24 Lang, 1995: 163.
25 Dorr, 1984, 1990, 1991; Ungoed-Thomas, 1997; Siraj-Blatchford, 1995; Erwin, 1996; Best, 1996; Weisinger, 1998; Collins, ca. 1996; Conaty, 1999.
26 Harvey-Jones, 1993:27.
27 Block, 1987:107.
28 Ibid., 189.
29 Harvey-Jones, 1993:24.
30 Burkan, 1996:78.
31 Frankl, 1974.
32 Handy and Aitken, 1990:125.
33 Stoltz, 1997:287.
34 Jackson, 1997:164 and Haydon, 1997.
35 Leigh and Maynard, 1995:56.
36 Wootton and Horne, 1997:64.
37 Block, 1987:105.
38 Nanus, 1992:27.
39 Belasco, 1990:99.
40 Ibid.,11.
41 Clayton, 1997:24.
42 Dobson and Starkey, 1993:11.
43 Woodward, 1994:119.
44 Mancini, 1994:57.
45 Ibid., 56.
46 Ibid., 57.
47 Finney, 1989:118.
48 Costello, 1994:17.
49 Finney, 1989118.
50 Bell, 1997:127-128
51 Pasmore, 1994:43-44.
52 Wellington, 1995:86.
53 Ungoed-Thomas, 1997:120.
54 Womack, Jones and Roos, 1990:25.

55 Ibid.
56 Wellington, 1995:87.
57 Dorr, 1990:124.
58 Ibid.
59 Lampikoski and Emden, 1996:102-104.
60 Scott and Jaffe, 1991:39 and Moss-Kanter, 1989.
61 Finney, 1989:127.
62 Lorriman, Young, and Kalinauckas, 1995:37.
63 Kotter, 1996:168.
64 Dobson and Starkey, 1993:120-121, see also Chetley, 1990.
65 Horne and Pierce, 1996:117.
66 Ibid.
67 Barnes, 1996:60.
68 Buchholz and Roth, 1987:89.
69 Pasmore, 1994:211-212.
70 MacBeath, 1998:118.
71 Halsall, 1998:57, see also Whitaker, 1997.
72 Leigh and Maynard, 1995 99, see also Nolan, 1987 and Maginn, 1994.
73 Eggert, 1996:68.
74 Russell, 1994:62.
75 Halsall, 1998:57.
76 Taylor and Thornton, 1995:45.
77 Ibid.
78 Taylor and Thackwray, 1997:64.
79 Johnson and Redmond, 1998:129.
80 Ibid., 1998:96.
81 Kamp 1997:3.
82 Ibid.
83 Cane, 1996:25.
84 Whiteley and Hessan, 1996:197.
85 Omhae, 1982:209.
86 Ibid., 210.
87 Stoltz, 1997:20-23.
88 Bowring-Carr and West-Burnham, 1997:149, see also Askew and Carnell, 1998. .
89 Burkan, 1996:78.
90 Handy, 1990:63.
91 Maister, 1997:99.

92 Swieringa and Wierdsma, 1992:33.
93 Dubrin, 1997:64.
94 Buchanan and Huczynski, 1997:299.
95 Cane, 1996:26-27.
96 Handy, 1993:118.
97 McIntyre, 1998:180.
98 Ibid.
99 Lampikoski and Emden, 1996:116.
100 Iacocca, 1985:53-54 see also Boyett and Conn, 1995:36-38.
101 Lagadec, 1993:14.
102 Cane, 1996:43.
103 Ibid.
104 Ibid., 55.
105 Wellington, 1995:97.
106 Mistéil, 1997:90.
107 Hale and Whitlam, 1995:118.
108 Johnson and Scholes, 1993:413.
109 Johnson and Redmond, 1998:96.
110 Ghoshal and Bartlett 1998:77.
111 Ibid. see also Kidd, Crawford and Riches, 1997.
112 Mistéil: 1997:89.
113 Barnes, 1996:59.
114 Ibid.
115 Ibid., 60.
116 Nanus, 1992:136, see also Crawley, 1995.
117 Senge et al, 1997:358.
118 Zuker, 1992:37, see also Blandford, 1997:70-71 and 200-201.
119 Ryan and Oestreich, 1991:77.
120 Ibid.
121 Benson, 1996:131.
122 Telford, 1996:58.
123 Ibid., 59.
124 Leigh and Maynard, 1995:120.
125 Ibid., 21.
126 Stoll and Fink, 1996:155.
127 Ibid.
128 Ibid., 160.
129 Clark, 1996, see also INTO Publication, 1993.
130 Hargreaves and Hopkins, 1991:3.

131 Hargreaves, 1994:261-262, see also Nias et al, 1992 and Stoll and Myers, 1998.

132 Ungoed-Thomas, 1997:131, see also Blandford, 1997.

133 Fullan and Hargreaves, 1992:50, see also Joyce et al, 1997.

134 Fullan and Hargreaves, 1992:108.

135 Block, 1987:86.

136 Fullan and Hargreaves, 1992:110-111 and Hopkins, Ainscow and West, 1994.

137 See Civil, 1997.

138 Washington, 1996:136, see also Fisher, 1996 and UNICEF 2000 and 2001.

139 See Rodd 1994; David 1998.

140 Freire, 1972:12, see also Kyriacou, 1995 and 1997.

141 See Mc Carthy, 1980; Prentice, 1996; Lealman, 1996.

142 Bruce, 1997:58.

143 Ibid., 203.

144 See Widlake, 1986; Comer, 1988; McAllister Swap, 1990a.

145 Whitaker, 1995:94, see also Goldman and Newman, 1998:1-24 and 113-168.

146 Whitaker, 1997:69.

147 Stoll and Fink, 1996:82.

148 Whitaker, 1997:71.

149 Ibid.

150 Ibid., 72.

151 Ibid.

152 Fullan, 1995:104.

153 Stoll and Fink, 1996:83.

154 Ibid., 84.

155 Whitaker, 1997:72.

156 Ibid. see also Crawford et al, 1997.

157 Hopkins, Ainscow and West, 1994:87.

158 Ibid.

159 Ibid.

160 Stoll and Fink, 1996:84.

161 Whitaker, 1997:74.

162 Ibid., 75.

163 Ibid., 76.

164 Ibid.

165 Bowring-Carr and West-Burnham, 1997:54.

166   Creese, 1995:35.
167   Preedy, Glatter, and Levacic, 1997:189.
168   Ibid.
169   Convention on the Rights of the Child - adopted by the General Assembly of the UN, 1989 and World Declaration and Plan of Action from the World Summit for Children, 1990.
170   Hart, 1997:45.
171   Ibid.
172   Ibid., 42.
173   Bagley, Woods and Glatter, 1996:125-138.
174   See Vincent, 1997.
175   Ibid., 45-57.
176   Ibid., 57-58.
177   Bernard van Leer Foundation, 1986:11, see also Coleman, 1998.
178   Ibid., 1988:7.

Chapter Six: Conclusions and Challenges

1   Conaty, 1999.
2   See Wilton, 1975:3-15.
3   Hatton, 1985:228.
4   Conaty, 1999:370-371.
5   Ibid., 195-212.
6   Ibid., 325-326.
7   Hargreaves, 1994:262.
8   Fullan and Stiegelbauer, 1991:235.
9   Stoll and Fink, 1996:133, see also Webb and Vulliamy, 1996:142-164.
10   Conaty, 1999:172-358, and 481-484
11   See Imich, 1994:3-11.
12   Hayden, 1997:122.
13   Ryan, 1999:52
14   Conaty, 1999:359-411.
15   Ibid., 1999:292-305, 316-320 and 359-411.
16   Ibid., 1999:359-411.
17   Dowling and Pound, 1994:69.
18   Pantin, 1979 and 1984.
19   Macbeth, 1995:51.

20   See Stoll and Fink, 1996:133-149.
21   Conaty, 1999:172-338.
22   Griffiths, 1998:21.
23   Conaty, 1999.
24   Ibid., 232-282.
25   Paz, 1990:53.
26   See endnote 45, Chapter Three
27   NAPS, 1997
28   Arango, ca.1989.
29   Department of Education, 2000.
30   See Ryan, 2001.
31   Grant, 1988.
32   Conaty, 1999.

Bibliography

Adair, J. *Effective Time Management: How to Save Time and Spend it Wisely*, London: Pan Books Ltd., 1988

Altrichter, H., Posch, P. and Somekh, B. *Teachers Investigate their Work: An Introduction to the Methods of Action Research*, London: Routledge, 1993

Anglin-Lawlor, A. *To School Through the Home: A Journey of Parental Participation in Education*, Maynooth: M.A. Thesis, 1994

Arango, M. *Involving Parents in the Participatory Process of Creating Appropriate Environments for the Healthy Development of Children at Risk: The Crucial Link Between Families and School*, Occasional Paper, The Hague: Bernard van Leer Foundation 1989ca.

Archer, P. 'Public Spending on Education, Inequality and Poverty' cited in Cantillon et al., *Rich and Poor: Perspectives on Tackling Inequality in Ireland*, Dublin: Oak Tree Press, 2001

Area Development Management Limited. *Integrated Local Development Handbook*, Dublin: ADM Ltd., 1995

Askew, S. and Carnell, E. *Transforming Learning: Individual and Global Change*, London: Cassell, 1998

Atkin, J. and Bastiani, J. with Goode, J. *Listening to Parents: An Approach to the Improvement of Home-School Relations*, Kent: Croom Helm Ltd.,1988

Atkinson, D. *Radical Urban Solutions: Urban Renaissance for City Schools and Communities*, London: Cassell, 1994a

Atkinson, D. *The Common Sense of Community*, London: Demos, 1994b

Avalos, B. 'Education for the Poor: Quality or Relevance?', *British Journal of Sociology of Education*, 13/4 (1992) 419-436

Bacik, I., and O'Connell, M. *Crime and Poverty in Ireland*, Dublin: Round Hall, Sweet & Maxwell, 1998

Bagley, C., Woods, P. and Glatter, R. 'Scanning the Market: School Strategies for Discovering Parental Perspectives', *Educational Management and Administration*, 24/2 (1996) 125-138

Barber, M. *Raising Standards in Deprived Urban Areas*, London: National Commission on Education Briefing No. 8, 1993

Barker, W. *Early Childhood Care and Education: The Challenge*, The Hague: Bernard van Leer Foundation, 1987

Barnes, T. *Kaizen Strategies for Successful Leadership: How to Take your Organization into the Future*, London: Pitman, 1996

Bastiani, J. *Working with Parents: A Whole School Approach*, Berkshire: NFER-Nelson, 1989

Bastiani, J. (ed.), *Parents and Teachers 1: Perspectives on Home School Relations*, Berkshire: NFER-Nelson, 1987

Bastiani, J. (ed.), *Parents and Teachers 2: From Policy to Practice*, Berkshire: NFER-Nelson,1988

Beattie, M. 'New Prospects for Teacher Education: Narrative Ways of Knowing Teaching and Teacher Learning', *Educational Research*, 37/1 (1995) 53-70

Belasco, J.A. *Teaching the Elephant To Dance: Empowering Change in Your Organization*, London: Century Business, 1992

Belbin, R.M. *The Coming Shape of Organization*, Oxford: Butterworth-Heinemann, 1998

Bell, L. 'Staff teams and Their Management' in Kydd, L., Crawford, M. and Riches, C. (eds.), *Leadership and Teams in Educational Management*, Buckingham: Open University Press, 1997

Bendure, G. and Friary, N. *Eastern Caribbean*, Victoria Australia: Lonely Planet Publications, 1994

Benson, J.F. *Working More Creatively With Groups*, London: Routledge, 1996

Bentley, T. *Motivating People: Sharpen Your Skills in Motivating People to Perform*, Cambridge: McGraw-Hill International UK Ltd., 1996

Bernard van Leer Foundation *Children and Community Progressing Through Partnership: Summary Report and Conclusions*, The Hague: Bernard van Leer Foundation, 1988

Bernard van Leer Foundation *Multi-Cultural Societies: Early Childhood Education and Care* (Summary Report and Conclusions), The Hague: Bernard van Leer Foundation, 1984

Bernard van Leer Foundation *The Parent as Prime Educator: Changing Patterns of Parenthood* (Summary Report and Conclusions), The Hague: Bernard van Leer Foundation, 1986

Bernard van Leer Foundation *Children at the Margin: A Challenge for Parents, Communities and Professionals*, The Hague: Bernard van Leer Foundation, 1987

Bernard van Leer Foundation *Where Have All the Fathers Gone?* The Hague: Bernard van Leer Foundation, 1992

Best, R. (ed.), *Education, Spirituality and the Whole Child*, London: Cassell, 1996

Blanchard, K., Carew, D., Parisi-Carew, E. *The One Minute Manager Builds High Performing Teams*, London: Fontana,1993

Blanchard, K., O'Connor, M. *Managing By Values,* San Francisco: Berrett-Koehler, 1997

Blandford, S. *Resource Management in Schools: Effective and Practical Strategies for the Self-Managing School,* London: Pitman, 1997

Blasé, J. and Blasé, J.R. *Empowering Teachers: What Successful Principals Do,* California: Corwin Press Inc., 1994

Block, P. *The Empowered Manager: Positive Political Skills At Work,* San Francisco: Jossey-Bass, 1987

Block, P. *Stewardship: Choosing Service Over Self-Interest,* San Francisco: Barrett-Koehler Publishers Inc., 1993

Bogdanowicz, M. *General Report on Parents Participation in the Education System in the Twelve Member States of the European Community* (Section 111), Brussels, 1994

Bourne, R. (ed.), *Crisis and Response: A Report of the Fourth International Community Educational Conference,* Leicester: ICEA, 1983

Bowring-Carr, C. and West-Burnham, J. *Effective Learning in Schools: How to Integrate Learning and Leadership for a Successful School,* London: Pitman Publishing, 1997

Boyett, J. and Conn, H. *Maximum Performance Management: How to Manage and Compensate People to Meet World Competition,* Oxford: Glenbridge Publishing Ltd., 1995

Bramley, P. *Evaluating Training Effectiveness: Translating Theory into Practice,* London: McGraw-Hill, 1991

Brantlinger, E. and Majd-Jabbari, M. 'The Conflicted Pedagogical and Curricular Perspectives of Middle-Class Mothers', *Journal of Curriculum Studies,* 30/4 (1998) 431-460

Bronfenbrenner, U. *A Report on Longitudinal Evaluation of Pre-School Programs-Volume 11: Is Early Intervention Effective? Washington: Department of Health Education and Welfare,* 1974 cited in Paz, R. *Paths to Empowerment: Ten Years of Early Childhood Work in Israel,* 1990

Brookfield, S. *The Skillful Teacher,* San Francisco: Jossey-Bass, 1990

Bruce, T. *Early Childhood Education,* London: Hodder and Stoughton, 1997

Bryk, A. and Driscoll, M. in Wehlage, G. Ruther, R. Smith, G. Lesko, N. and Fernandez, R. *Reducing The Risk: Schools As Communities Of Support,* Sussex: The Falmer Press, 1989

Buchanan, K. and Huczynski, A. *Organizational Behaviour,* Hempsted Hertfordshire: Prentice Hall Europe, 1997

Buchholz, S. and Roth, T. *Creating the High-Performance Team,* New York: Wiley and Sons, Inc., 1987

Burkan, W. *Wide Angle Vision,* New York: John Wiley and Sons Inc., 1996

Burke, S. *Youth as a Resource: Promoting the Health of Young People at Risk,* Dublin: A Report of the National Consultative Committee on Health Promotion, 1999

Byrne, B. *Bullying: A Community Approach,* Dublin: Columba Press, 1994

Caldwell, J. and Spinks, M. *The Self-Managing School,* Lewes, East Sussex: The Falmer Press, 1988

Cane, S. *Kaizen Strategies For Winning Through People: How to Create a Human Resources Program for Competitiveness and Profitability,* London: Pitman Publishing, 1996

Catterall, J. 'Risk and Resilience in Student Transitions to High Schools,' American Journal of Education, 106/2 (1998) 302-333

Cattermole, J. and Robinson, N. 'Effective Home/School Communication from the Parents' Perspective,' *Phi Delta,* 6/1 (1985) 48-50

Chen, C. and Stevenson, H. 'Homework: A Cross-cultural Examination,' *Child Development,* 60/3 (1989) 551-561

Chetley, A. *The Power to Change,* The Hague: Bernard van Leer Foundation, 1990

Civil, J. *Managing People Effectively,* London: Ward Lock, 1997

Civil, J. *Leadership Skills for Success*, London: Ward Lock, 1997a

Clark, D. *Schools as Learning Communities: Transforming Education*, London: Cassell, 1996

Clark, R. 'Critical Factors in Why Disadvantaged Students Succeed or Fail in School?' in Johnston, J. and Borman, K. (eds.), *Effective Schooling For Economically Disadvantaged Students: School Based Strategies for Diverse Student Populations*, 1992

Clayton, S. *Sharpen Your Team's Skills in Supervision*, Maidenhead, Berkshire: McGraw-Hill, 1996

Clayton, S. *Sharpen Your Team's Skills in Developing Strategy*, Maidenhead, Berkshire: McGraw-Hill, 1997

Clegg, D. and Billington, S. *Leading Primary Schools: The Pleasure, Pain and Principles of Being a Primary Headteacher*, Buckingham: Open University Press, 1997

Cohen, R. *Shaping Tomorrow: The Servol Programmes in Trinidad and Tobago*, The Hague: Bernard van Leer Foundation, 1991

Coleman, P. Parent, *Student and Teacher Collaboration: The Power of Three*, California: Corwin Press,Inc., 1998

Collins, U. *Developing A School Plan: A Step by Step Approach*, Dublin: Marino Institute of Education, 1996ca.

Comer, J.P. *School Power: Implications of An Intervention Project*, New York: Free Press, 1980

Comer, J.P. 'Educating Poor Minority Children', *Scientific American*, 259/5 (1988a), 24-30

Comer, J.P. Maggie's *American Dream: The Life and Times of a Black Family*, New York: New American Library, 1988b

Comer, J.P. 'Parent Participation in Schools,' *Phi Delta Kappan*, 67/6 (1986) 442-446

Commission on Local Governance, *Our Global Neighbourhood*, Oxford: Oxford University Press, 1995

Conaty, C. *Partnership in Education, through Whole School Development with Parent and Community Involvement: A Study of a National Initiative to Combat Educational Disadvantage –*

the Home, School, Community Liaison Scheme (2 Vols), NUI Maynooth: Ph.D. Thesis, 1999

Conaty, C. 'The Home, School, Community Liaison Scheme', *Journal of The Institute of Guidance Counsellors,* Vol. 24, Maynooth: Spring, 2000

Conference of Major Religious Superiors (CMRS) *Education and Poverty: Eliminating Poverty in the Primary School Years,* Dublin: CMRS 1992

Coolahan, J. (ed.), *Report on the National Education Convention,* Dublin: The Convention Secretariat, 1994

Corson, D. *Changing Education For Diversity,* Bristol: Open University Press, 1998

Costello, S.J. *Management: Effective Performance,* Burr Ridge, Illinois: Business One Irwin/Mirror Press, 1994

Council of Europe *The European Convention on Human Rights,* Strasbourg, 1984

Covey, S.R. *The Seven Habits Of Highly Effective People: Powerful Lessons in Personal Change,* London: Simon and Schuster Ltd., 1992

Covey, S.R., Merrill, A.R. and Merrill *First Things First: To Live, To Love, To Learn, To Leave a Legacy,* London: Simon and Schuster Ltd., 1994

Craig, I. 'Training Needs of Primary Headteachers,' *Educational Management and Administration,* 10/1 (1982) 17-22

Craig, S. *Community Participation: A Handbook For Individuals and Groups in Local Development Partnerships,* Dublin: Combat Poverty Agency, 1995a

Craig, S. *Making Partnership Work: A Handbook on Involvement in Local Development Partnership,* Dublin Combat Poverty Agency, 1995b

Crawford, M., Kydd, L. and Riches, C. *Leadership and Teams in Educational Management,* Buckingham: Open University Press, 1997

Crawley, J. *Constructive Conflict Management: Managing To Make A Difference,* London: Nicholas Brealey Publishing, 1995

Creese, M. *Effective Governors Effective Schools: Developing the Partnership,* London: David Fulton Publishers Ltd., 1995

Cropley, A. 'Lifelong Learning: A Rationale for Teacher Training,' *Journal of Education for Teaching,* 7/1 (1981) 57-89

Cross, C. 'National Goals: Four Priorities for Educational Researchers,' *Educational Researcher,* 19/8 (1990) 21-24

Crowley, N. and Watt, P. 'Local Communities and Power' in Caherty, T., Storey, A., Gavin, M., Molloy, M., Ruane, C. (eds.), *Is Ireland A Third World Country?* Beyond the Pale Publications, 1992

Cullen, B. *Integrated Services and Children At Risk,* Dublin: Combat Poverty Agency, 1997

Cullingford, C. *The Effective Teacher,* London: Cassell, 1995

Cusick, P. and Wheeler, C. 'Educational Morality and Organizational Reform,' *American Journal of Education,* 96/2 (1988) 231-290

Dalin, P. with Rolff, H. G. and Kleekamp, B. *Changing The School Culture,* London: Cassell, 1993

David, T. *Researching Early Childhood Education: European Perspectives,* London: Chapman, 1998

Davies, D. 'Schools Reaching Out: Family, School, and Community Partnerships for Student Success,' *Phi Delta Kappan,* 72 (1991) 376-382

de Jong, F. 'The Relationship Between Students' Behaviour at Home and Attention and Achievement in Elementary School', *British Journal of Educational Psychology,* 63/2 (1993) 201-213

Delgado-Gaitan, C. 'Involving Parents in the Schools: A Process of Empowerment', *American Journal of Education,* 100/1 (1991) 20-46

Delgado-Gaitan, C. and Allexsaht-Snider, M. *Mediating School Cultural Knowledge For Children: The Parents' Role* in Johnston, J. and Borman, K. (eds.), *Effective Schooling For Economically Disadvantaged Students: School-Based Strategies For Diverse Student Populations,* Norwood, New Jersey: Ablex Publishing Corporation, 1992

Department of Education *Curriculum* 1971

Department of Education Report of the Primary Education Review Body, Dublin: Stationery Office, 1990

Department of Education Parents as Partners in Education: Circular 24/91 and Circular M27/91, Dublin: Department of Education, 1991

Department of Education *Education for a Changing World:* Green Paper Ireland 1992, Dublin: Stationery Office, 1992

Department of Education 'The Basic Principles of the HSCL Scheme', Dublin: Department of Education, 1993

Department of Education *Position Paper on Regional Educational Councils,* Dublin: Department of Education, 1994

Department of Education *Charting Our Education Future: White Paper on Education,* Dublin: The Stationery Office, 1995

Department of Education Memorandum, Dublin: Department of Education, 1990

Department of Education Explanatory Memorandum, Dublin: Department of Education, 1991

Department of Education Interim Report 1, Dublin: Department of Education, 1992

Department of Education National Coordinators' Annual Report, Dublin: Department of Education, 1993

Department of Education National Coordinators' Annual Report, Dublin: Department of Education, 1994

Department of Education Message from the Minister (foreward) in The Board of Management: A Guide for Parents, Dublin: National Parents Council-Primary, 1993

Department of Education Support Teacher Service, Dublin: Department of Education, 1998

Department of Education Review of Department's Operations, Systems and Staffing Needs, Dublin: Cromien Report, 2000

Diggins, P., Doyle, E., Herron, D. *Whole School Development: Taking Ownership of the Process,* Dublin: Drumcondra and West Dublin Teachers Centres, 1996

Dobson, P. Starkey, K. *The Strategic Management Blueprint,* Oxford: Blackwell, 1993

Donthwaite, R. *The Growth Illusion: How Economic Growth Has Enriched the Few, Impoverished the Many, and Endangered the Planet,* Dublin: Lilliput Press Ltd., 1992

Dorr, D. *Spirituality and Justice,* Dublin: Gill and Macmillan Ltd., 1984

Dorr, D. *Integral Spirituality: Resources for Community, Justice, Peace and the Earth,* Dublin: Gill and Macmillan Ltd., 1990

Dorr, D. *The Social Justice Agenda: Justice, Ecology, Power and the Church,* Dublin: Gill and Macmillan Ltd., 1991

Dowling, E. and Osborne, E. (eds.), *A Joint Systems Approach to Problems with Children,* London: Routledge, 1994

Dowling, E. and Pound, P. Joint Interventions with Teachers, Children and Parents in the School Setting, in Dowling, E. and Osborne, E. (eds.), *The Family and The School: A Joint Systems Approach to Problems with Children,* London: Routledge, 1994

Drudy, S. and Lynch, K. *Schools and Society in Ireland,* Dublin: Gill and Macmillan Ltd., 1993

Drudy, S. and Uí Chatháin, M. *Gender Equality in Classroom Interaction,* NUI Maynooth: Department of Education, 1999

Dubrin, A. *Leadership,* New York: Alpha Books, 1997

Dulles, A. *Models of the Church,* Dublin: Gill and Macmillan, 1987

Earley, C. and McKenna, G. *Actions Speak Louder: A Source Book for Social Ministry,* Dublin: Columba Press, 1987

Edwards, V. and Redfern, A. *At Home in School*, London: Routledge, 1988

Eggert, M.A. *Managing Your Appraisal*, Alresford: Management Pocketbooks Ltd., 1996

Elder, S. *The Power of the Parent* cited in Yale (incomplete information), 1990

Elliott-Kemp, J. and Elliott-Kemp, N. *Managing Change and Development in Schools*, Essex: Longman Group UK Ltd., 1992

Epstein, J.L. 'What Principals Should Know About Parent Involvement,' *Principal*, 66/3 (1987) 6-9

Epstein, J.L. Toward a Theory of Family-School Connections: Teacher Practices and Parent Involvement in Hurrelmann, K., Kaufman, F. and Losel, F. (eds.), *Social Interventions: Potential and Constraints*, 121-136, New York: Walter de Gruyter, 1987

Ericson, D., and Elleth, F. 'Taking Student Responsibility Seriously,' *Educational Researcher*, 19/9 (1990) 3-10

Erwin, E. J. (ed.), *Putting Children First: Visions for a Brighter Future for Young Children and Their Families*, Baltimore, Maryland: Brookes Publishing Co., 1996

European Commission *Teaching and Learning: Towards a Learning Society*, Luxembourg: Office for Official Publications of the EU, 1995

European Community *European Convention on Human Rights* Strasbourg, 1984

European Union. *Education and Initial training Systems in the European Union*, Luxembourg: Office for Official Publication of the European Communities, 1995

Evans, J.L. Effectiveness: The State of the Art in Bernard van Leer Publication, *Early Childhood Matters*, The Hague: BvLF, 1998

Ferder, F. and Heagle, J. *Partnership: Women and Men in Ministry*, Notre Dame: Ave Maria Press, 1989

Finney, J. *Understanding Leadership*, London: Daybreak, Darton

Longman and Todd Ltd., 1989

Fisher, J. *Starting from the Child?*, Buckingham: Open University Press, 1996

Flanagan, N., Hasse, T. and Walsh, J. *Planning For Change: A Handbook on Strategic Planning for Local Development Partnerships*, Dublin: Combat Poverty Agency, 1995

Frankl, V.E. *Man's Search for Meaning: An Introduction to Logo Therapy*, London: Hodder and Stoughton Ltd., 1974

Freire, P. *Pedagogy of the Oppressed*, London: Penguin, 1972

Freire, P. *Pedagogy Of Hope: Reliving Pedagogy of the Oppressed*, New York: The Continuum Publishing Company, 1997

Freire, P. *Paulo Freire on Higher Education: A Dialogue At the National University of Mexico*, New York: State University of New York, 1994

Freire, P. and Shor, I. *A Pedagogy for Liberation*, London: Macmillan, 1987

Fullan, M. *Change Forces: Probing the Depths of Educational Reform*, London: Falmer Press, 1995b

Fullan, M. and Hargreaves, A. *What's Worth Fighting for in Your School?* Buckingham: Open University Press, 1992

Fullan, M. and Stiegelbauer, S. *The New Meaning of Educational Change*, London: Cassell Educational Ltd., 1991

Fullan, M.G. *Successful School Improvement*, Buckingham: Open University Press, 1995a

Galloway, D., Rogers, C., Armstrong, D., Leo, E. *Motivating the Difficult to Teach*, Essex: Addison Wesley Longman Ltd., 1998

Gardner, H. *Frames of Mind: The Theory of Multiple Intelligences*, London: Harper-Collins, 1993

Gaster, L., Smart, G., Harrison, L., Forrest, R. and Stewart, M. *Interim Evaluation of the Ferguslie Park Partnership*, Edinburgh: the Scottish Office Central Research Unit, 1995

Geldard, K. and Geldard, D. *Counselling Children: A Practical Introduction*, London: Safe Publications, 1997

Ghoshal, S. and Bartlett, C.A. *The Individualized Corporation: A Fundamentally New Approach To Management*, London: Henemann, 1998

Goldman, G. and Newman, B. *Empowering Students to Transform Schools*, California: Corwin Press Inc., 1998

Goode, J. Parents as Educators, in Bastiani, J. (ed.), *Parents And Teachers 1: Perspectives on Home-School Relations*, Berkshire: NFER-Nelson, 1987

Gordon, W. and Langmaid, R. *Qualitative Market Research*, Brookfield USA: Gower Publishing Ltd., 1988

Gray, J. and Wilcox, B. *Good School, Bad School: Evaluating Performance and Encouraging Improvement*, Buckingham: Open University Press, 1995

Griffiths, M. *Educational Research for Social Justice: Getting Off the Fence*, Buckingham: Open University Press, 1998

Hale, R. and Whitlam, P. *The Power of Personal Influence*, Maidenhead, Berkshire: McGraw-Hill Book Company Europe, 1995

Hall, C. and Lindzey, G. *Theories of Personality*, New York: John Wiley and Sons, Inc. 1957

Halliday, J. *Back to Good Teaching: Diversity Within Tradition*, London: Cassell, 1996

Halsall, R. (ed.), *Teacher Research and School Improvement: Opening Doors From The Inside*, Buckingham: Open University Press, 1998

Handy, C. *The Age of Unreason*, London: Arrow, 1990

Handy, C. *Understanding Organizations: A New Edition of This Landmark Study*, London: Penguin, 1993

Handy, C. and Aitken, R. *Understanding Schools As Organizations*, London: Penguin, 1990

Hannan, D., Smyth, E., McCullagh, J., O'Leary, R. and McMahon, D. *Coeducation and Gender Equality*, Dublin: Oak Tree Press, 1996

Hargreaves, A. *Changing Teachers, Changing Times: Teachers' Work and Culture in the Post-Modern Age*, London: Cassell, 1994

Hargreaves. A., Earl, L. and Ryan, J. *Schooling for Change: Reinventing Education for Early Adolescents*, London: Falmer Press, 1997

Hargreaves, D. H., Hopkins, D. *The Empowered School: The Management and Practice of Development Planning*, London: Cassell, 1996

Harris, A., Jamieson, I. and Russ, J. *School Effectiveness and School Improvement: A Practical Guide*, London: Pitman Publishing, 1996

Harris, C. *Networking for Success: The NLP Approach to a Key Business and Social Skill*, Dublin: Oak Tree Press, 2000

Hart, R.A. *Children's Participation: The Theory and Practice of Involving Young Citizens in Community Development and Environmental Care*, London: Earthscan, 1997

Harvey-Jones, J. *Managing to Survive: A Guide To Management Through The 1990's*, London: Heinemann, 1993

Hatton, E. 'Team Teaching and Teacher Orientation to Work: Implications for the Preservice and Inservice,' *Journal of Education for Teachers*, 11/3 (1985) 228-244

Hatton, E., Munns, G. and Dent, J. 'Teaching Children in Poverty? Three Australian Primary School Responses,' *British Journal of Sociology of Education*, 17/1 (1996) 39-52

Hatwood-Futrell, M. 'Restructuring Teaching: A Call for Research,' *Educational Researcher*, 15/10 (1986) 5-8

Hayden, C. *Children Excluded from Primary School: Debates, Evidence, Responses*, Buckingham: Open University Press, 1997

Haydon, G. *Teaching About Values: A New Approach*, London: Cassell, 1997

Haynes F. *The Ethical School: Consequences, Consistency, Care, and Ethics*, London: Routledge, 1998

Hayton, A. *Tackling Disaffection and Social Exclusion: Education Perspectives and Policies,* London: Kogan Page, 1999

Healy, S. *The Rural Development School: Towards A Vision Of Rural Ireland,* Dublin: RTE Education Department, 1992

Henerson, M. E., Lyons Morris, L. and Fitz-Gibbon, C.T. *How to Measure Attitudes,* California: Sage, 1987

Hill, D., and Cole M. *Schooling and Equality: Fact, Concept and Policy,* London: Kogan Page, 2001

Hirshaman, A. *Exit, Voice and Loyalty: Responses to Decline in Firms, Organizations, and States,* Cambridge Mass.: Harvard University Press, 1970

Hope, Timel, and Hodzi, *Training for Transformation: A Handbook for Community Workers,* Zimbabwe: Mambo Press, 1984

Hopkins, D., Ainscow, M. and West, M. *School Improvement in an Era Of Change,* London: Cassell, 1994

Horne, H. and Pierce, A. *A Practical Guide to Staff Development and Appraisal in Schools,* London: Kogan Page, 1996

Iacocca, L. with Novak, W. *Iacocca: An Autobiography,* London: Biddles of Guilford for Sidgwick and Jackson Ltd., 1995

Imich, A. 'There Is No Evidence that Exclusions Lead to Improvement in Pupil Behaviour,' *Educational Research,* 36/1 (1994) 3-11

Irish Government and European Social Fund Evaluation Report: *ESF and the Local Urban and Rural Development Operational Programme,* Dublin: ESF Evaluation Unit, 1999

Irish Government. *White Paper on Educational Development,* Dublin: Stationery Office, 1980

Irish Government. *Partnership 2000 for Inclusion, Employment and Competitiveness,* Dublin: Stationery Office, 1996

Irish Government. *Sharing in Progress: National Anti-Poverty Strategy,* Dublin: Stationery Office, 1997ca.

Irish Government. *Early School Leavers and Youth Unemployment:*

Forum Report No. 11, Dublin: National Economic and Social Forum 1997a

Irish Government. *The Constitution of Ireland,* Dublin: Government Publications, 1937

Irish Government. *Rural Renewal – Combating Social Exclusion:* Forum Report No. 12, Dublin: National Economic and Social Forum 1997b

Irish Government. Education Act, Dublin: Stationery Office, 1998

Irish Government. Education (Welfare) Act, Dublin: Stationery Office, 2000

Irish Government. *Strengthening Families for Life: Final Report to the Minister for Social, Community and Family Affairs,* Dublin: Stationery Office, 1998

Irish Government. *Annual Report of the Inter-Departmental Policy Committee,* Dublin: The Stationery Office, 1999

Irish Government. *Ireland's National Report on the Implementation of the Outcome of the UN World Summit for Social Development,* Dublin: Stationery Office, 2000

Irish Government. *Our Children – Their Lives:* National Children's Strategy, Dublin: Stationery Office, 2000

Irish Government. *Ireland: National Development Plan 2000 – 2006,* Dublin: Stationery Office, 2000

Irish National Teachers' Organisation, (INTO) *The Professional Development of Teachers: Issues in Inservice Education,* Dublin: INTO, 1993

Jackson, D. *Dynamic Organisations: The Challenge of Change,* London: Macmillan Press Ltd., 1997

Johnson, G., Scholes, K. *Exploring Corporate Strategy,* Hempstead, Hertfordshire: Prentice Hall International, 1993

Johnson, R., Redmond, D. *The Art of Empowerment: The Profit and Pain of Employee Involvement,* London: Financial Times and Pitman Publishing, 1998

Johnston, H. and O'Brien, T. *Planning for a More Inclusive Society:*

An Initial Assessment of the National Anti-Poverty Strategy, Dublin: Combat Poverty Agency, 2000

Johnston, J. and Borman, K. *Effective Schooling for Economically Disadvantaged Students: School-Based Strategies for Diverse Student Populations,* New Jersey: Ablex, 1992

Joyce, B., Calhoun, E., and Hopkins, D. *Models of Learning – Tools for Teaching,* Philadelphia: Open University Press, 1997

Joyce, B., Calhoun, E., and Hopkins, D. *The New Structure of School Improvement: Inquiring Schools and Achieving Students,* Philadelphia: Open University Press, 1999

Jung, C. G. *Aion: Researches into the Phenomenology of the Self,* London: Routledge, 1959

Kamp, D. *Sharpen Your Team's Skills in People Skills,* Maidenhead, Berkshire: McGraw-Hill, 1997

Kellaghan, T., Weir, S., Ó hUallacháin, S. and Morgan, M. *Educational Disadvantage in Ireland,* Dublin: Department of Education, Combat Poverty Agency, Educational Research Centre, 1995

Kellaghan, T. and Greaney, B. *The Educational Development of Students Following Participation in a Pre-School Programme in a Disadvantaged Area in Ireland,* The Hague: Bernard van Leer Foundation, 1993a

Kellaghan, T., Sloane, K., Alverez, B. and Bloom, B. *The Home Environment and School Learning: Promoting Parental Involvement in the Education of Children,* San Francisco, California: Jossey-Bass, 1993

Kotter, J. P. *Leading Change,* Boston: Harvard Business School Press, 1996

Krasnow, J. *Building Parent-Teacher Partnerships: Prospects from the Perspective of the Schools Reaching Out Project,* Boston: Institute for Responsive Education, 1990a

Krasnow, J. *Improving Family-School Relationships: Teacher*

Research from the Schools Reaching Out Project, Boston: Institute for Responsive Education, 1990b

Krumm, V. 'Expectations About Parents in Education in Austria, Germany and Switzerland' in Macbeth, A. and Ravn, B. (eds.), *Expectations About Parents In Education: European Perspectives,* 1994

Kydd, L., Crawford, M. and Riches, C. *Professional Development for Educational Management,* Buckingham: Open University Press, 1997

Kyriacou, C. *Essential Teaching Skills,* Cheltenham: Stanley Thornes Publishers Ltd., 1995

Kyriacou, C. *Effective Teaching in Schools: Theory and Practice,* Cheltenham: Stanley Thornes Publishers Ltd., 1997

Lagadec, P. *Preventing Chaos in a Crisis: Strategies For Prevention, Control And Damage Limitation,* Maidenhead, Berkshire: McGraw-Hill, 1993

Lampikoski, K. and Emden, J.B. *Igniting Innovation: Inspiring Organizations by Managing Creativity,* Chichester: John Wiley and Sons, 1996

Lang, P. 'The Place of Social and Personal Education in the Primary School' in Siraj-Blatchford, J. and I. (eds.), *Educating The Whole Child: Cross Curricular Skills, Themes and Dimensions,* Buckingham: Open University Press, 1995

Lareau, A. 'Gender Differences in Parent Involvement in Schooling', in Wrigley, J. (ed.), *Education and Gender Equality,* London: Falmer Press, 1992

Lealman, B. *The Whole Vision of the Child,* in Best, R. *Education, Spirituality and the Whole Child,* London: Cassell, 1996

Leigh, A. and Maynard, M. *Leading Your Team: How to Involve and Inspire Teams,* London: Nicholas Brealey Publishing Ltd., 1995

Lindon, J. *Equal Opportunities in Practice,* London: Hodder and Stoughton, 1998

Lomax, P. (ed.), *Quality Management in Education: Sustaining the Vision Through Action Research*, London: Routledge, 1996

Lorriman, J., Young, R. and Kalinauckas, P. *Upside Down Management: Revolutionizing Management and Development to Maximize Business Success*, Maidenhead Berkshire: McGraw-Hill, 1995

Lovett, T. (ed.), *Radical Approaches to Adult Education: A Reader*, London: Routledge, 1988

Lumby, J. 'Planning in Further Education: The Business of Values,' *Educational Management and Administration*, 27/1 (1999) 71-83

Lynch, K. *The Hidden Curriculum: Reproduction in Education, A Reappraisal*, Wiltshire: The Falmer Press, 1989

Maastricht Treaty 1992

MacBeath, J. *Success Against the Odds: Effective Schools in Disadvantaged Areas*, London: Routledge, 1996

MacBeath, J. I Didn't Know He Was Ill: the Role and Value of the Critical Friend in Stoll, L. and Myers. K, (eds.), *No Quick Fixes: Perspectives on Schools in Difficulty*, London: Falmer Press, 1998

MacBeath, J. *Schools Must Speak For Themselves: The Case for School Self-Evaluation*, London: Routledge, 1999

MacBeath, J. (ed.), *Effective School Leadership: Responding to Change*, London: Chapman Publishing Ltd., 1998

MacBeath, J., Mearns, D. and Smith, M. *Home from School*, Glasgow: Jordanhill College of Education, 1986

Macbeth, A. *The Child Between: A Report on School-Family Relations in the Countries of the European Community* (Studies Collection: Education Series no. 13), Brussels: Commission of the European Communities, 1984

Macbeth, A. *Involving Parents: Effective Parent-Teacher Relations*, Oxford: Heinemann Educational, 1989

Macbeth, A. and Ravn, B. *Expectations About Parents In Education: European perspectives,* Glasgow: Computing Services Glasgow University, 1994

Macbeth, A., McCreath, D. and Aitchison, J. (eds.), *Collaborate or Compete?: Education Partnerships in a Market Economy,* London: Falmer Press, 1995

Mackinnon, D., Newbould, D., Zeldin, D. and Hales, M. *Education in Western Europe: Facts and Figures,* London: Hodder and Stoughton Educational, 1997

Macleod, F. (ed.), *Parents and Schools: The Contemporary Challenge,* East Sussex: The Falmer Press, 1989

Maginn, M.D. *Effective Teamwork,* Burr Ridge: Business One Irwin/Mirror Press, 1994

Maister, D.H. *True Professionalism: The Courage To Care About Your People, Your Clients, And Your Career,* New York: Free Press, 1997

Mancini, M. *Time Management,* Burr Ridge: Business One Irwin/Mirror Press, 1994

Marshall, C. and Rossman, G.B. *Designing Qualitative Research,* London: Sage Publications, 1995

Martinez, R., Marques, R. and Souta, L. 'Expectations About Parents in Portugal and Spain' in Macbeth, A. and Ravn, B. (eds.), *Expectations About Parents In Education: European Perspectives,* Glasgow: Computing Services Glasgow University, 1994

Mathison, S. 'Why Triangulate', *Educational Researcher,* 17/2 (1988) 13-17

Mc Court, F. *Angela's Ashes: A Memoir of a Childhood,* London: Flamingo, 1997

Mc Intyre, M. *The Management Team: Five Key Strategies for Maximising Group Performance,* San Francisco: Jossey-Baas, 1998

Mc Laughlin, W. and Irby, A. 'Urban Sanctuaries:

Neighbourhood Organizations that Keep Hope Alive,' *Phi Delta Kappan* (1994) 300-306

McAllister Swap, S. *Parent Involvement and Success for All Children: What We Know Now.* Boston: Institute for Responsive Education, 1990a

McAllister Swap, S. *Schools Reaching Out and Success for All Children: Two Case Studies,* Boston: Institute for Responsive Education, 1990b

McCarthy, B. *The Four Mat System: Teaching to Learning Styles with Right /Left Mode Technique,* Barrington IL: Exel, Inc., 1980

McNiff, J. *Action Research: Principles and Practices,* London Routledge, 1992

Mezirow, J. *Fostering Critical Reflection in Adulthood,* Oxford: Jossey-Bass, 1990

Mezirow, J. *Transformative Dimensions of Adult Learning,* London: Jossey-Bass, 1991

Mezirow, J. *Adult Education and Empowerment for Individual and Community Development in Radical Learning for Liberation,* Maynooth: Centre for Adult and Community Education, 1996

Midwinter, E. Community Education in Craft, M., Raynor, J., Cohen, L., *Linking Home and School: A New Review.* London: Harpes & Row, 1980

Mistéil, S. *The Communicator's Pocketbook,* Alresford: Management Pocketbooks Ltd., 1997

Mortimore, P., Sammons, P., Stoll, L., Lewis, D., and Ecob, R. *School Matters: The Junior Years,* London: P. Chapman Publishing Ltd. 1995

Mortimore, P. and Little, V. *Living Education: Essays in honour of John Tomlinson,* London: Chapman Publishing Ltd., 1997

Moss-Kanter, M. *When Giants Learn to Dance: Mastering the Challenges of Strategy, Management, and Careers in the 1990s,* London: Thomson Business Press, 1989

Moxley, D., Najor-Durak, A., and Dumbrigue, C. *Keeping Students in Higher Education: Successful Practices and Strategies for Retention*, London: Kogan Page, 2001

Mueller, D.J. *Measuring Social Attitudes: A Handbook for Researchers and Practitioners*, New York: Teachers College Press, 1986

Mufson, L., Cooper, J. and Hall, J. 'Factors Associated with Underachievement in Seventh-Grade Children,' *Journal of Educational Research*, 38/1 (1989) 5-10

Nanus, B. *Visionary Leadership*, San Francisco: Jossey-Bass Publishers, 1992

National Academy of Education 'Research and the Renewal of Education,' *Educational Researcher*, 20/6 (1991) 19-22

National Parents Council-Primary: The Board of Management: *A Guide for Parents*, Dublin: National Parents Council-Primary, 1993

Nias, J., Southworth, G. and Campbell, P. *Whole School Curriculum Development in the Primary School*, London: Falmer Press, 1992

Nimnicht, G. Arango, M. with Hearn, L. *Meeting the Needs of Young Children: Policy Alternatives*, The Hague: Bernard van Leer Foundation, 1987

Nisbet, J. and Watt, J. *Educational Disadvantage: Ten Years On*, Edinburgh: Her Majesty's Stationery Office, 1984

Nolan, V. *Teamwork*, London: Sphere Books Ltd., 1987

O'Callaghan, J.B. *School-Based Collaboration with Families: Constructing Family-School-Agency Partnerships that Work*, San Fransisco: Jossey-Bass Publishers, 1993

O'Connor, C.A. *The Handbook For Organizational Change: Strategy and Skill for Trainers and Developers*, London: McGraw-Hill, 1993

O'Donnell, C. *Ecclesia: A Theological Encyclopedia of the Church*, Minnesota: The Liturgical Press, 1996

OECD Reviews of National Policies for Education: Ireland, Paris: Organisation for Economic Co-operation and Development, 1991

OECD Our Children At Risk, Paris: Organisation for Economic Cooperation and Development, 1995

OECD Co-ordinating Services for Children and Youth at Risk: A World View, Paris: Centre for Educational Research and Innovation, Organisation for Economic Co-operation and Development, 1998

Ohmae, K. *The Mind of the Strategist: The Art Of Japanese Business*, New York: McGraw-Hill, Inc., 1982

Open University, The *Deprivation, Disadvantage and Compensation: Education Studies*, A Second Level Course E202, Schooling and Society, London: Ebenezer Baylis and Son Ltd., 1997

O'Sullivan, D. 'Teachers' views on the Effects of the Home,' *Educational Research* 22/2 (1980) 138-142

Pallas, A., Natriello, G. and McDill, E. 'The Changing Nature of the Disadvantaged Population Current Dimensions and Future Trends,' *Educational Researcher*, 18/5 (1989) 16-22

Pantin, G. *A Mole Cricket Called Servol: The Early Years of an Education and Community Development Project in the West Indies*, The Hague: Bernard van Leer Foundation, 1979

Pantin, G. *The Servol Village: A Caribbean Experience in Education and Community*, The Hague: Bernard van Leer Foundation, 1984

Pasmore, W.A. *Creating Strategic Change: Designing the Flexible, High-Performing Organization*, New York: John Wiley and Sons, Inc., 1994

Paz, R. *Paths to Empowerment: Ten Years of Early Childhood Work in Israel*, The Hague: Bernard van Leer Foundation, 1990

Pedersen, E., Faucher, T. and Eaton, W. 'A New Perspective on the Effects of first-Grade Teachers on Children's Subsequent Adult Status,' *Harvard Educational Review*, 48/1 (1978) 1-31

Philip, H. and Chetley, A. *A Small Awakening*, the Hague: Bernard van Leer Foundation, 1988

Phillips, N. *Motivating for Change: How to Manage Employee Stress*, London: Pitman Publishing, 1995

Pignatelli, F. *Partnership in Education*, Conference Keynote Speech, Dublin, April 3rd, 1992, Dublin: CMRS, 1992

Porter, M.E., Takeuchi H. and Sakakibara, M. *Can Japan Compete?* London: Macmillan Press Ltd., 2000

Preedy, M., Glatter, R. and Levacic (eds.), *Educational Management: Strategy Quality and Resources*, Buckingham: Open University Press, 1997

Prentice, R. *The Spirit of Education: A Model for the Twenty-First Century*, in Best , R. *Education, Spirituality and the Whole Child*, London: Cassell 1996

Proctor, N. 'Towards a Partnership with Schools,' *Journal of Education for Teaching*, 10/3 (1984) 219-232

Prosser, J. *School Culture*, London: Chapman Publishing Ltd., 1999

Pugh, G. and De'Ath, E. *Working Towards Partnership in the Early Years*, London: National Children's Bureau, 1989

Rae, L. *How To Measure Training Effectiveness*, Hampshire: Gower, 1997

Ravn, B. *Expectations About Parents in Education in Scandinavian Countries* in Macbeth, A. and Ravn, B. (eds.), *Expectations About Parents In Education: European Perspectives*, Glasgow: Computing Services Glasgow University, 1994

Reay, D.G. *Evaluating Training*, London: Kogan Page, 1994

Resnik, L. 'Learning In School and Out,' *Educational Researcher*, 16/9 (1987) 13-20

Riley, K.A. *Whose School is it Anyway?* London: Falmer Press, 1998

Roberts, K. *Linking Home and School: A New Review,* cited in Craft, M., Raynor, J., Cohen, L. London: Harper & Row, 1980

Robertson, P. *Partnership for Progress: The Mid-Term Evaluation of The Home School Employment Partnership,* Glasgow: University of Strathclyde, 1995

Rodd, J. *Leadership in Early Childhood,* Buckingham: Open University Press, 1994

Roland-Martin, J. 'A Philosophy of Education for the Year 2000', *Phi Delta Kappan,* (1995) 355-359

Rosenholtz, J. 'Effective Schools: Interpreting the Evidence' *American Journal of Education,* 93 (1985) 352-388

Ruane, C. 'Solidarity: A Two-Way Process', in Caherty, T., Storey, A., Gavin, M., Molloy, M., Ruane, C. (eds.), *Is Ireland A Third World Country?* Belfast: Beyond the Pale Publications, 1992

Russell, T. *Effective Feedback Skills,* London: Kogan Page, 1994

Rutherford, B. and Billig, S. 'Eight Lessons of Parent, Family, and Community Involvement in the Middle Grade,' *Phi Delta Kappan,* (1995) 64-68

Ryan, C. 'Early School Leaving: A Sharing of Responsibility', cited in *Issues in Education,* Volume 4, Dublin: ASTI Education Journal, 1999

Ryan, C. *The Perpetual Paradox: Opening Doors of Opportunity for Children 'At Risk', A Study of a National Initiative to Combat Early School Leaving – The 8 to 15 Early School Leaver Initiative,* NUI, Maynooth: M.A. Thesis, 2001

Ryan, K.D. and Oestreich, D.K. *Driving Fear Out of the Workplace: How to Overcome the Invisible Barriers to Quality, Productivity and Innovation,* San Francisco: Jossey-Bass Inc., 1991

Ryan, S. *Evaluation of a Home-School-Community Liaison Scheme in Irish Elementary Schools,* Kalamazoo: Western Michigan University, 1996

Ryan, S. *The Home-School-Community Liaison Scheme: Final Evaluation Report*, Dublin: Educational Research Centre, 1994

Salach, S. *In the First Person Plural: Growing Up with a Disadvantaged Community*, The Hague: Bernard van Leer Foundation, 1993

Sallis, J. *Schools, Parents and Governors: A New Approach to Accountability*, London: Routledge, 1988

Salole, G. *Building on People's Strengths: The Case For Contextual Child Development*, The Hague: Bernard van Leer Foundation, 1992

Scaparro, F. 'Expectations About Parents in Education: An Italian Point of View' in Macbeth, A. and Ravn, B. (eds.), *Expectations About Parents In Education: European Perspectives*, 1994

Schön, D.A. *Education the Reflective Practitioner: Towards a New Design for Teaching and Learning in the Professions*, San Francisco: Jossey-Bass, 1987

Schorr, L.B. *Parent Involvement and Success for All Children: What We Know Now*, cited in McAllister Swap, S. Boston: Institute of Responsive Education, 1990a

Schorr, L.B. *Within Our Reach: Breaking the Cycle of Disadvantage*, London: Doubleday, 1988a

Schweinhart, L.J. *What the High/Scope Perry Preschool Study Reveals about Developmental Transitions and Contextual Challenges of Ethnic Males*, Paper presented at the Annual Meeting of the American Psychological Association, Ontario, 1993

Scott, C.D. and Jaffe D.T. *Empowerment: Building a Committed Workforce*, London: Kogan Page Ltd, 1991

Scottish Office *New Life for Urban Scotland*, H.M. Government, 1998

Seashore-Louis, K. and Kruse, S. *Professionalism and Community:*

Perspectives on Reforming Urban Schools, California: Corwin Press, Inc., 1995

Seeley, D. *Education Through Partnership: Mediating Structures and Education,* Cambridge, Massachusetts: Ballinger Publishing Company, 1981

Senge, P.M., Kleiner, A., Roberts, C., Ross, R.B. and Smith, B.J. *The Fifth Discipline Fieldbook: Strategies and Tools for Building a Learning Organization,* London: Nicholas Brealey, 1997

Sergiovanni, J.J. *Building Community in Schools,* San Francisco: Jossey-Bass Publishers, 1994

Sergiovanni, J.J. *Leadership for the Schoolhouse: How Is It Different? Why Is It Important?* San Francisco: Jossey-Bass Inc., 1996

Sheppard, C. *What Can Agencies Outside the Education Service Contribute?* In Hayden, C. *Children Excluded from Primary School: Debates, Evidence, Responses,* Buckingham: Open University Press, 1997

Short, G. 'Teacher Expectations and West Indian Underachievement,' *Educational Research* 27/2 (1985) 95-101

Short, P., Greer, T. and Melvin, W. 'Creating Empowered Schools: Lessons in Change,' *Journal of Educational Administration,* 32/4 (1994) 38-58

Siraj-Blatchford, J. and I. (eds.), *Educating the Whole Child: cross-curricular skills, themes and dimensions,* Buckingham: Open University Press, 1995

Smit, F. and van Esch, W. Opportunities for Parents to Influence Education in the Netherlands in Macbeth, A. and Ravn, B. (eds.), *Expectations About Parents In Education: European Perspectives,* Glasgow: Computing Services University of Glasgow, 1994

Smyth, E. *Do Schools Differ?: Academic and Personal Development Among Pupils in the Second-Level Sector,* Economic and Social Research Institute, 1999

South, S. and Crowder, K. 'Escaping Distressed Neighbourhoods: Individual, Community and Metropolitan Influences,' *American Journal of Sociology*, 102/4 (1977) 1040-1084

Stewart, R. *The Reality of Management*, London: Pan Books, 1985

Stoll, L. and Fink, D. *Changing Our Schools: Linking School Effectiveness and School Improvement*, Buckingham: Open University Press, 1996

Stoll, L. and Myers, K. *No Quick Fixes: Perspectives on Schools in Difficulty*, London: Falmer Press, 1998

Stoltz, P.G. *Adversity Quotient: Turning Obstacles into Opportunities*, New York: John Wiley and Sons Inc., 1997

Swieringa, J., Wierdsma, A. *Becoming a Learning Organization: Beyond the Learning Curve*, Workingham: Addison-Wesley, 1992

Taylor, G. and Thornton, C. *Managing People*, London: Directory of Social Change, 1995

Taylor, P. and Thackwray, B. *Managing for Investors in People*, London: Kogan Page, 1997

Taylor, W. *Linking Home And School: A New Review*, cited in Craft, M., Raynor, J., and Cohen, L. London: Harper and Row, 1980

Telford, H. *Transforming Schools through Collaborative Leadership*, London: Falmer Press, 1996

Testerman, J. 'Holding At-Risk Students: The Secret Is One-on-One,' *Phi Delta Kappan* (1996) 364-365

Thomson, C. 'A Community Work Approach in Adult Education', *International Journal of Lifelong Education*, 13/3 (1991) 181-196

Tinto, V. *Leaving College, Rethinking the Causes and Cures of Student Attrition*, Chicago: University of Chicago Press, 1993

Tizard, B. and Hughes, M. *Young Children Learning*, London: Fontana, 1984

Tizard, J., Schofield, W. and Hewison, J. 'Collaboration Between Teachers and Parents in Assisting Children's Reading,' *British Journal of Educational Psychology* 52/1 (1982) 1-15

Topping, K. and Wolfendale S. *Parental Involvement in Children's Reading*, Kent: Croom Helm Ltd., 1985

Troyer, L. and Younts, C. 'Whose Expectations Matter? The Relative Power of First- and Second- Order Expectations in Determining Social Influence,' *American Journal of Sociology* 103/3 (1997) 692-732

Ungoed-Thomas, J. *Vision of a School: The Good School in the Good Society*, London: Cassell, 1997

United Nations Children's Fund (UNICEF) *First Call for Children: World Declaration and Plan of Action from the World Summit for Children*, New York: UNICEF 2000

United Nations Children's Fund (UNICEF) *Convention on the Rights of the Child*, New York: UNICEF 2000

United Nations Children's Fund, (UNICEF) *The State of the World's Children 2001: Early Childhood*, New York: UNICEF House, 2001

United Nations Children's Fund, (UNICEF) *The State of the World's Children 2002: Leadership*, New York: UNICEF House, 2002

Vincent, C. *Parents and Teachers: Power and Participation*, London: Falmer Press, 1996

Washington *Creating An Ideal World for Children*, in Erwin, J. *Putting Children First: Visions of a Brighter Future for Young Children and Their Families*, Baltimore: Brookes Publishing, 1996

Watt, J. 1989 *Community Education and Parental Involvement: A Partnership in Need of a Theory*, Sussex: The Falmer Press.

Webb, R., Vulliamy, G. *Roles And Responsibilities In The Primary School: Changing Demands, Changing Practices*, Buckingham: Open University Press, 1996

Weber, M. *The Theory of Social and Economic Organization*, New York: Free Press, 1947

Wehlage, G., Rutter, R., Lesko, N. and Fernandez, R. *Reducing the Risk: Schools as Communities of Support*, Sussex: Falmer, 1989

Weisinger, H. *Emotional Intelligence at Work: The Untapped Edge for Success*, San Francisco: Jossey-Bass, 1998

Welling, W. Family Education Conference in Coventry 1985 cited in *Family Education Conference Report*, Coventry: Community Education Development Centre, 1988

Wellington, P. Kaizen *Strategies for Customer Care: How to Create a Powerful Customer Care Program- and Make it Work*, London: Pitman, 1995

Whalley, M. *Learning To Be Strong: Setting Up a Neighbourhood Service for Under-Fives and Their Families*, Kent: Hodder and Stoughton, 1994

Whitaker, P. *Managing to Learn: Aspects of Reflective and Experiential Learning in Schools*, London: Cassell, 1995

Whitaker, P. *Primary Schools and The Future: Celebration, Challenges And Choices*, Buckingham: Open University Press, 1997

Whitehead, J. Foreward in McNiff, J. Action Research: *Principles And Practices*, London: Routledge, 1995

Whitehead, J. and Eaton Whitehead, E. *Promise of Partnership: Leadership and Ministry In An Adult Church*, San Francisco: Harper, 1991

Whiteley, R. and Hessan, D. *Customer Centered Growth: Five Proven Strategies for Building Competitive Advantage*, London: Century Business, 1996

Widlake, P. *How to Reach the Hard to Teach*, Stony Stratford: Open University Press, 1985

Widlake, P. *Reducing Educational Disadvantage*, Stratford: Open University Press, 1986

Widlake, P. and Macleod, F. *Raising Standards: Parental*

Involvement Programmes and the Language Performance of Children, Coventry: Community Education Development Centre, 1984

Wills, M. *Managing the Training Process: Putting the Basics into Practice*, London: McGraw-Hill, 1993

Wilton, V. 'A Mother Helper Scheme in the Infant School,' *Educational Research*, 18/1 (1975) 3-15

Wolfendale, S. *Parental Participation in Children's Development and Education*, London: Gordon and Breach Science Publishers, 1983

Wolfendale, S. *Empowering Parents and Teachers: Working for Children*, London: Biddles Ltd., 1992

Womak, J.P., Jones, D.T. and Roos, D. *The Machine That Changed The World*, New York: Simon and Schuster, 1990

Woodward, H. and Beckman Woodward, M. *Navigating Through Change*, Burr Ridge: Irwin, 1994

Wootton, S. and Horne, T. *Strategic Planning: The Nine Step Programme*, London: Logan Page, 1997

Wrigley, J. *Education and Gender Equality*, London: Falmer Press 1995

Wright, R.J. *Beyond Time Management: Business with Purpose*, Boston: Butterworth-Heinemann, 1997

Yánez, T. *Venezuela: Developing Inter-Sectorial Networks*, in Bernard van Leer Publication, Childhood Matters, The Hague: BvLF, 1998

Youngman, M. 'Six Reactions to School Transfer,' *British Journal of Educational Psychology* 48/1 (1978) 280-289

Zeichner, K. and Liston, D. *Reflective Teaching*, New Jersey: Lawrence Erlbaum Associates, 1996

Zuker, E. *The Seven Secrets of Influence*, New York: McGraw-Hill, Inc., 1991